Puffin Books

CREEPY-CRAWL

Spiders, centipedes,
poles . . . the world o   .....s is a fascinating
one that never ceases to be a source of amazement. It
is inhabited by the strangest creatures, some well
known but often misunderstood, others rarely seen
and little thought of.

But here is your chance to become an expert on all
sorts of creepy-crawlies: how much can a caterpillar
eat? How does a maggot see? Does a millipede really
have 1000 legs? *Creepy-Crawlies* is packed with in-
formation, and full of safe, simple and fun activities
designed to reveal even more secrets of these extra-
ordinary creatures – see for yourself how a snail
moves, watch a tadpole slowly transform itself into a
frog, or turn an axolotl into a salamander!

Beginning with common creatures that are easily
studied, the book progresses on to those that require
more care or are more difficult to obtain. Finally, for
the real enthusiast, there are some of the strangest
creepy-crawlies, including axolotls and cockroaches.

Whether at home or at school, *Creepy-Crawlies* will
provide hours of entertainment as well as valuable
insight into the natural world.

Paul Temple is the author of *How to Grow Weird and
Wonderful Plants* and, with Ralph Levinson, *How to
Make Square Eggs*, a book of zany science experiments. He trained as a biologist before becoming a
teacher. He is now a management consultant and
trainer.

PAUL TEMPLE

Illustrated by Jane Cope

PUFFIN BOOKS

PUFFIN BOOKS

Published by the Penguin Group
27 Wrights Lane, London w 8 5 t z, England
Viking Penguin Inc., 40 West 23rd Street, New York, New York 10010, U S A
Penguin Books Australia Ltd, Ringwood, Victoria, Australia
Penguin Books Canada Ltd, 2801 John Street, Markham, Ontario, Canada l 3 r 1 b 4
Penguin Books (N Z) Ltd, 182–190 Wairau Road, Auckland 10, New Zealand

Penguin Books Ltd, Registered Offices: Harmondsworth, Middlesex, England

First published 1988

Made and printed in Great Britain by
Cox and Wyman Ltd, Reading, Berks
Filmset in Linotron Trump Medieval by
Rowland Phototypesetting Ltd, Bury St Edmunds, Suffolk

Acknowledgements

Several people helped me in the writing of this book. My father first taught me to watch small animals rather than attack them. Diane Hibberd and the children of Strand-on-the-Green Junior School deserve most of the credit for the idea of the book. Jane Marchant, Sandra Banfield and my parents gave suggestions for animals to include. As always Sandra Banfield did the typing. Finally, Dawn Richardson and Mark Dolan arranged for some original entertainment. To all of them – thank you.

Contents

Introduction

Welcome to the wonderful world of the creepy-crawlies. It is a place that is often hidden from us but which is full of the most amazing animals. Some of them, like the beautiful ladybird, are creatures most people like and recognize. Others, like the leaf insect, can look rather frightening at first. However, all creepy-crawlies have one thing in common. They are creatures that most people know very little about. Ask yourself a few questions.

- What does a ladybird like to eat for lunch?
- Can snails swim?
- Is a tarantula spider really deadly?

Do you know the answers? No? Well, don't worry because you soon will. After you have read this book you will be able to find all sorts of interesting creatures wherever you look, and you will know how many of them like to spend their fascinating lives.

The first part of the book describes some animals that are very easy to work with. This means they are easy to find or buy, no trouble to look after and very simple to learn about. None the less, they are still very interesting and fun, so it is a good idea to start keeping them to get used to looking after such small creatures. It will make the other animals in the book more fun to learn about because you will then have some experience of handling creepy-crawlies.

Nearer the middle of the book the animals described are more difficult, either to find or to work with. Towards the back of the book are described some of the strangest creepy-crawlies of all, including animals found mainly in tropical countries, which are often called 'exotics'. They are animals that need lots of care and attention. However, they are really very strange and incredible and so they will certainly be animals you will want to know about. Of course, you may not be able to keep some of these exotic animals at home but I know you will still enjoy learning about them. Why not ask your school teacher to start a mini-zoo. That way not only you but all your friends will be able to see these incredible creepy-crawlies.

As you will see, most of the animals can be found easily if you know where to look. A few, especially the exotics, will need to be bought. A section at the back of the book will help you find out where to buy these creepy-crawlies and their food. There is also a list of some interesting places that you might like to visit if you live in Britain.

Treat these creatures kindly and you will really enjoy getting to know them. They are strange animals to keep as pets, but when you understand them you will soon learn to like them. Then, the next time you unexpectedly bump into a small, wriggly, slimy creature you will smile instead of running away screaming 'eeek!'

Bluebottles

It may seem strange, but almost all of the animals you would think of straight away as creepy-crawlies are quite closely related. If you look at them you will find many of them share one common feature – they have six legs. These six-legged animals are called insects and are found anywhere that any animals can live, from the edges of the Arctic and Antarctic to the middle of deserts. There are even some that live on the oceans. Now although these insects are all similar they can be separated into different types. For instance, later in the book you will read about two different groups of insects, ants (with their close relatives, the termites) and beetles (such as ladybirds and cockroaches). First though, let's take a look at a group of insects that we all know and often dislike, the flies.

Flies are insects that use wings to move from one place to another. They have wings all their adult life and, unlike beetles, do not have a cover to protect the wings when they are not being used. There are two types of fly. Some have two pairs of wings while others have only one pair. In this case we are going to look at bluebottles, and you can spend some time trying to find out how many wings they have. The answer is given in the 'Did You Know' section.

Bluebottle will do as a general name but what we are really talking about are large houseflies. At first they may not appear very interesting but there are always questions worth asking. Have you ever wondered how a fly lands on the ceiling? Funny, isn't it? Does it fly along close to the ceiling, catch hold with its two front feet, brake very hard with its wings and suddenly do a somersault, still holding on with its feet (cartoon 1)? Does it do a loop-the-loop to end up flying upside down so it can just 'land' on the ceiling (cartoon 2)? Or does it do a gentle roll instead (cartoon 3)? Whichever it does, it all happens so quickly I doubt that you'll be able to see it.

Of course, just as fascinating is how the fly actually uses its feet to stick to a wall or ceiling. You can't find this out for yourself because the secret can be revealed only by looking at the feet with a very powerful microscope. If you did do this, you would see a very thin leg ending in a large flat pad. The pad is covered in hooked hairs and shallow grooves. Although the hooked hairs are able to hold on to rough surfaces, this does not explain how a fly sticks to smooth surfaces like glass. This is where the grooves are important. They are always damp and can change shape slightly which means they can act as suckers. Thus the fly can hold on to glass by suction.

While we are on the subject, the foot is one of the parts of the insect that is responsible for the fly being described as dirty. Flies are not usually fussy eaters and houseflies are the least fussy of all. They will eat any food that is rotting or which is liquid enough to suck up. They don't care if the food has been on the

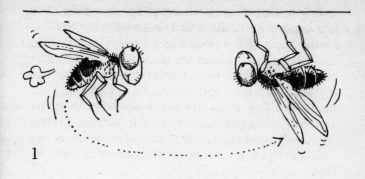

1

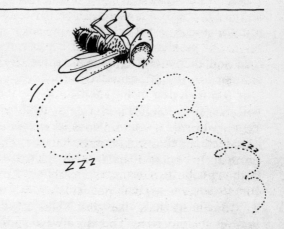

2

3

floor, in a dustbin, in a sewer or anywhere else. Obviously these sorts of places are bound to contain lots of germs. Some of these germs stick to their feet until they fly into a house and land on food waiting to be eaten by us. They don't deliberately use our food as doormats to wipe their feet on. It's like you walking in the country all day in a pair of shoes and then coming home and forgetting to take them off. All the dust and dirt is trodden into the floor of the house. So flies leave all those germs to live and grow in our food, ready to be eaten by us.

Sometimes when a fly lands on our food it finds it difficult to suck the food up, especially if it is something nice and sweet but solid like sugar. The fly solves the problem very simply. It just spits on the food and then sucks it up with some of the food dissolved in it. Unfortunately for us, that spit contains germs living inside the fly and some of them will stay on the food long after the fly has flown away. Yeuch! The germs sometimes cause simple illnesses like stomach aches, but really serious illnesses can be spread by houseflies so they are considered dangerous in many countries, especially those with a tropical climate and low hygiene standards.

What a nasty little creature a housefly is then, but they are not as horrible as baby houseflies which we call maggots. Even the word is ugly and very few people like to see them wiggling about in true creepy-crawly style. They live wherever there is food so, like flies, they will be found anywhere, however dirty, happily eating away at anything soft and rotting.

Now that you are really revolted at the thought of a maggot, you may be surprised to see an experiment using them. It just goes to prove that true scientists have to put aside their feelings in order to find out the truth. But don't worry, the maggots we use will be very clean and free of germs and diseases.

Do Maggots Like Light?

You will need
    2 portable lights
    2 pencils
    a few live maggots

some pieces of graph paper
a watch or clock with a second hand

What to do
Put a light by one side of the graph paper. Put the other lamp on one of the other three sides. Switch them on so that the lights shine towards the middle of the paper. Use a pencil to put a small mark and the word 'START' in the middle of the paper, and put an 'X' on each edge of the paper near the lights to show their positions.

Now pick up a lovely, wiggly maggot (buy these from fishing shops but DO NOT BUY COL-OURED MAGGOTS AS THEY CAN BE POISONOUS) and put it on the mark in the centre of the paper, with both lights still on. Using the watch or clock, time the maggot and every fifteen seconds mark the paper just behind the maggot's tail with the pencil. Put a 1 by the first mark, a 2 by the second mark, and so on. Do this for up to ten minutes or until the animal leaves the paper. Join all the dots with a line (follow the numbers starting from the middle).

Now give the maggot a rest or take another one. Start again but use a fresh piece of paper and only one light. Note the position of the light by drawing an 'X' on the edge of the paper nearest to the light. Mark the maggot's position every fifteen seconds for up to ten minutes, putting a 1 by the first mark, a 2 by the second, and so on as before.

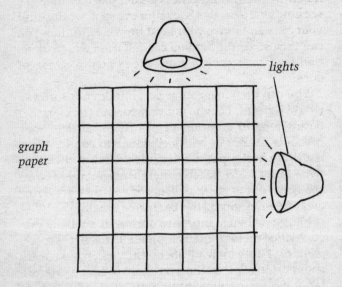

lights

graph
paper

When finished, put the maggot back and join all the dots with a line (follow the numbers starting from the middle). Do you notice anything about the direction in which the maggot moves? You should and I hope before you read on you try to think why anything you have noticed has happened. What you should find is that wherever you put the lights (marked by the Xs), the maggots always wander around a bit and then find the best way to go to get away from the light. In other words, maggots don't like light.

They can detect it using a dark coloured spot, not really an eye but a very primitive attempt at one, at the front or blunt end of the body. They wriggle away from light because they can be easily seen in it and might be eaten. The dark is a safer place to hide. To see how well a maggot's 'eye' (or eye spot) works, shut your eyes and move your head from side to side. You can't see anything but you can tell from which direction the light comes in much the same way a maggot does.

You can keep maggots as pets but I'm not sure you would want to. They're not very good at tricks, rather boring (not to mention ugly) to look at, and they certainly cannot be considered nice to handle. They really are better put in the garden when you've seen what they can do, but do remember to put them down carefully, out of the way. Ugly or not, they are living creatures and should not be treated cruelly.

Maggots change into flies during an amazing process called metamorphosis (pronounced *met-a-more-foe-sis*). You can read about this when you learn about caterpillars in the next chapter. Like a caterpillar, the maggot must spend some time inside a hard case. At this stage of the life cycle the maggot transforms into a pupa (*pew-pah*). Inside the case the fly pupa will grow legs and wings while the body changes shape.

Did You Know

- Houseflies (which include bluebottles) can carry at least thirty different types of disease, from those that cause just a slight tummy-ache to some that can kill.

- Some bluebottles aren't blue. They are green.

- Most flies lay eggs but some can give birth to live maggots.

- Houseflies, including bluebottles, have two wings.

2 Caterpillars

You will already know from the description of bluebottles that animals with six legs are insects. Well, here then is another insect but it isn't easy to see just six legs. The caterpillar is in fact a baby butterfly or moth and the adult does have six, and only six, legs. However, caterpillars have a few more! If you can take a close look you will see that they have six legs close together at the front. These are the true legs. At the back end there are some more sucker legs that help the animal to hold on or walk. These legs aren't the true legs and look very different from those at the front. Have a look at them and see if you can spot the differences.

If ever there was a creature that you could call a walking stomach surely the caterpillar must be it. All it does and all it is meant to do is eat. Just imagine, the creature wakes up in the morning, chomps on a leaf or two for breakfast, moves on to a few more leaves as a snack before lunch and as soon as they have been swallowed, what a bit of luck, it's time for lunch! Life is day after day of continuous gluttony lasting from breakfast to bedtime. Come to think of it, does a caterpillar ever sleep? Why not try to find caterpillars at night and see if they are eating or sleeping.

Why does a caterpillar need to eat so much? Believe it or not, the food is essential if the caterpillar is to get a good sleep. In the animal world sleep is a very complicated thing. First of all, nobody knows quite

why animals do sleep although it is known that most animals have to sleep for at least part of their lives. Another surprise is that there are several different types of sleep.

Human sleep is not such an incredible event. All we do is slow down our bodies a little, but there are surprisingly few changes and almost all of the body keeps working at quite near to normal speed. The next level of sleep is known by the complicated name of aestivation (ees-tea-vay-shun). In this type of sleep the body of the animal is drastically slowed down by a very big drop in body temperature. It's almost as if it went to sleep covered in ice except that it doesn't need ice because it just stops keeping its body warm. Animals that aestivate do so often, an excellent example being bats which do so once every twenty-four hours.

A third group of animals lower their body temperature for longer than bats. Instead of doing it for part of each day they do so for many days in a row, often for weeks or months on end. This is known as hibernation and, as with the other two types of sleep, saves energy which, in a cold winter when food is difficult or impossible to find, allows animals such as bears and squirrels to survive without eating, asleep until the weather warms up and food can be found. (Animals can wake up from hibernating during the winter but usually go back to sleep again soon. Squirrels often wake up in this way.)

The types of sleep we have looked at so far save energy so food is not needed in enormous amounts. Yes, animals that hibernate do eat a lot to store as fat so they can survive their winter sleep, but their appetites do not match that of the caterpillar. Caterpillar sleep is different again and is called metamorphosis. The process begins when the fat caterpillar stops eating. The caterpillar begins to produce a silk thread which it uses to build a chamber or cocoon (*cuh-coon*). The cocoon hardens with the caterpillar, now a pupa, inside. Cocoons can often be found stuck under leaves but a few caterpillars do make theirs on or under the ground. Although the caterpillar does appear to slow down, in reality it does the opposite and suddenly speeds up. Metamorphosis is one of the marvels of the natural world. While appearing to be asleep the little caterpillar will change from a wiggly, worm-like creature into a butterfly or moth which will soon hatch out and fly away. You can watch all this happen at home by keeping a few caterpillars as pets as described further on.

Once the butterfly or moth has hatched, it has to survive the first few most dangerous moments of its new life. For in these first few minutes its wings are crumpled and quite useless. Blood must be pumped into them so that they can take on their proper shape. Until the wings are flat they cannot be used to fly and so the butterfly can easily be caught by other animals for a tasty meal. If the wings are 'pumped up' then the butterfly can begin its real work which is to create more butterflies by reproduction.

Males and females must find each other so that they can mate and produce eggs. After mating the female will lay the eggs, often under leaves so that the baby caterpillars will hatch out near their food. The babies eat their egg cases first (if they do not, they will not grow properly) and so begin their incredible early life of gluttony. Of course, the adult butterflies eat to gain enough energy to live and reproduce but the effort is nothing like that of metamorphosis so their appetite is not as big (except in a few special cases). Adults usually eat nectar or decaying food, both of which are liquids and easy to suck up through the

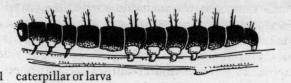

1   caterpillar or larva

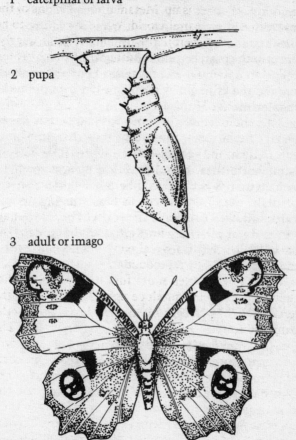

2   pupa

3   adult or imago

The three stages in the life of a butterfly

long mouth that is normally kept coiled out of the way. Tropical varieties of butterfly often drink water which contains a lot of salt.

Caterpillars are the young or larvae (*lar-vee*) of butterflies and moths. Because they eat enormous amounts of food, they are usually considered pests and killed by farmers and gardeners. The adult butterflies and moths are often spectacularly beautiful and have, in the past, been killed for butterfly collections. Many are now very rare because of butterfly collecting and the killing of caterpillars. Do not kill butterflies or moths at all. Help to protect and conserve them so that everyone can enjoy them as they flutter about in the open air. Collect small numbers of caterpillars and set them free when they become adult butterflies. If you have a garden, a small bit hidden at the back should be left wild so that the plants these insects need (such as stinging nettles) can be allowed to grow. Then you will be able to look forward to even more butterflies in the garden, and they'll eat the weeds rather than your garden plants.

How To Keep Caterpillars

You will need

a glass or plastic aquarium
some old net curtain
some caterpillars or eggs

a length of elastic
a pair of scissors
a regular supply of fresh leaves

or

a cardboard box with top

some clear cellophane
a ruler

a pencil a pair of scissors
glue or sticky tape a regular supply of
some old net curtain fresh leaves
some caterpillars or
eggs

What to do

Begin by building their home. If you can get a plastic
or glass aquarium then you only need to make the
top. To do this get some fine mesh or net curtain (the
holes must be smaller than the baby caterpillars) and
cut a piece to cover the open top of the aquarium. BE
CAREFUL WITH THE SCISSORS! Take a piece
of elastic that will go all around the aquarium. Cut it
so that it is about 2cm shorter. Tie the two ends
together and use this as an elastic band to hold the net
on as a lid.

If you do not have an aquarium find a cardboard box
at least the size of a shoe box, although it can be any
shape and as large as you want. Decide which of the
longest sides is going to be the front of the cage. Don't
choose the smaller ends, the lid or the bottom of the
box. Use a pencil and ruler to draw a rectangle on the
front. It should be slightly smaller than the front,
leaving a margin all the way round of about 2cm.
Now cut along the line you've drawn so that the piece
of card can be taken out to leave a large hole in the
front.

ASK AN ADULT TO HELP OR WATCH YOU
AS SCISSORS CAN BE VERY DANGEROUS.

Now cut a piece of cellophane that is just smaller
than the whole front of the box but bigger than the
piece you cut out. Stick or tape this over the hole on

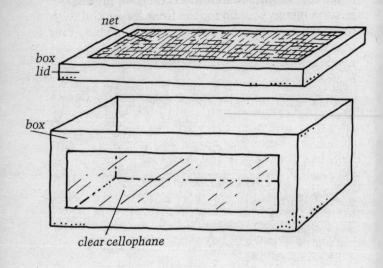

net

box
lid

box

clear cellophane

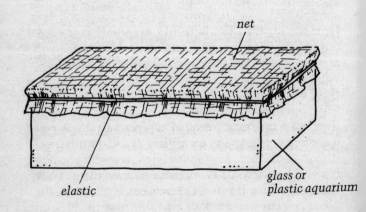

net

elastic

glass or
plastic aquarium

the inside of the box so that you make a window. To make the lid cut out another rectangular hole in the box-top just as you did for the front. **Be careful with those scissors**. Then cut a piece of mesh or net curtain that is bigger than the hole you have made. Stick it inside the lid to cover the hole completely. Your cage is now ready.

Collect some caterpillars or eggs. In the tropics these can be found all year round. In other places they are found just after the warm weather begins (in spring) and butterflies appear in gardens. The eggs look like tiny barrels and are usually stuck to the underside of leaves. If you find any, do also take some of the leaves and remember which type of plant they are. You will need plenty of fresh leaves later to feed the caterpillars. If you cannot find any caterpillars or eggs you may wish to buy them. See the back of the book for suppliers.

Now all you need to do is put the cage containing the animals and food into a light, warm place but not in direct sunlight. You can watch your eggs hatch, the caterpillars grow, the process of pupation and the fantastic sight of the butterfly eventually crawling out of the pupa case and pumping up its wings. If you are successful and have many butterflies or moths, you can keep a few and hope they lay eggs. If you do this, do provide fresh twigs with several healthy leaves on so the butterflies can choose where to lay as they are amazingly fussy. Whatever you do, if you collected wild eggs or caterpillars, let all your butter-flies go so they can be enjoyed by everyone. If you buy tropical butterflies you will have to keep them. They will not survive if you set them free.

Did You Know

- There are vampire moths! They live by sucking the blood of other animals.

- The male Emperor moth can smell a female from as far away as 11km (about 6 miles).

- The pretty wings of butterflies are not brightly coloured. They reflect light but in doing so they cause something very similar to a rainbow, but with some of the colours missing.

- The North American Monarch butterfly migrates every year from North America to Mexico. Their journey can be 3000 miles and they have successfully flown across the Atlantic Ocean.

- The biggest eater in the world of caterpillars is a peculiar American moth. In two days the caterpillar munches so much food (compared with its own weight) that to equal it you would have to eat about sixteen million hamburgers (with the bread rolls) in two days.

- Butterflies have been found flying at a height of almost 6km (19,000').

- Female butterflies produce a smelly chemical that says, 'here I am, come and get me' to any male butterfly. The males use their antennae to smell the chemical and follow it to wherever the female is. The chemicals are called pheromones (*feromones*) and are so strong that a single drop the size of a pin-head can be found by a male butterfly or moth that is several kilometres away.

Woodlice

Every now and then you come across an animal that really isn't what you might expect it to be. Here we have an example of one that at a quick look appears to be a beetle. It isn't though. This little creature is related to animals that would usually be expected to live in the sea, but it prefers land. Read on to discover what other surprises it has up its sleeve (or perhaps up its shell?).

The woodlouse is a marvellous example of an animal that has existed for millions of years without changing. It could easily be described as a living tank with lots of legs and seems brilliantly designed to survive the searching of hungry and bigger animals. A closer look will show a lot more. Woodlice are in fact related to shrimp, crabs and lobsters that, unlike it, are found in the ocean. They are crustaceans (*crustay-shuns*) and, in common with all other crustaceans, not only have a shell and ten legs but also need to stay fairly close to water.

If you look more closely at the shell of the woodlouse, you will see that it is divided into several separate pieces that link together or overlap to form a layer of protective plates. The shell plates are very strong and slightly curved so that when trodden on, either deliberately or accidentally, the animal is very likely to survive. (Don't try this as they aren't strong enough to protect the woodlouse from you.) There is a soft spot though. If a hungry animal can overturn the woodlouse, its soft underbelly would not only be exposed, but it would also provide an easy way to a nice juicy meal (that is nice, if you like the taste of raw woodlouse!). Fear not though, for the able little creature has a neat trick to help it survive. As soon as the belly is exposed the woodlouse rolls itself up into a tight little ball, leaving only the hard plates exposed, and most hunters prefer to try elsewhere rather than chew through the plates.

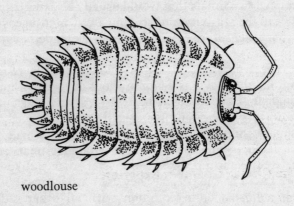

woodlouse

Underneath the shell there is something else of interest. All animals breathe air and so do crustaceans, but they can only obtain their air when it has been dissolved in water. Just as fish do this with special organs known as gills, so do woodlice. The gills are hidden by the shell because they are very fragile and need to be protected. They are therefore very difficult to see, but they force the animals to seek out damp places in order that the gills remain moist and absorb air. You will be able to prove that woodlice always head for damp spots with an easy experiment which follows.

So woodlice like water but what else do they like? For a start, they prefer to live in cracks and crevices where they can feel themselves in contact with their surroundings, with both their legs and back touching something. And of course you will realize that cracks are likely to be dark, so it seems that woodlice like to live in dark, damp crevices such as under stones or between the bark and wood of rotting trees – in fact, in exactly the places you would expect a creepy-crawly to hide in. Food is usually very easy to find as any dead and rotting vegetable matter can be eaten. This means that they are useful animals to us, helping to clear up the mess when plants die. Fortunately they do not bite or sting, so despite their rather strange appearance they are harmless. Now for an experiment to find out if woodlice really do like what we accused them of liking.

The Choice Chamber Experiment

You will need

some stiff cardboard
a ruler
4 elastic bands
some water
some woodlice

pencil or pen
scissors
some sticky tape
about 8 (2cm) pieces of
    dry, thin stick
a jam jar or plastic tub

What to do

A 'choice chamber' is a box that allows some wood-lice (or any other animal you are experimenting with) to choose to move to one of several positions, and by seeing which one is chosen we can tell which conditions are preferred. To make the choice chamber copy the figure on page 27 on to your cardboard and then cut out the shape you have drawn. Use the back of the scissors to score along all the dotted lines so that it will be easy to fold the card. (Whenever you use the scissors MAKE SURE YOU ASK AN ADULT TO WATCH OR HELP YOU as they can be very dangerous, especially when scoring lines.) Lay the card on a flat surface and fold the card up so that pairs of letters join together (A will meet A, B will meet B and so on) until eventually the box looks complete and is loosely held together. Hold the box together using the four elastic bands and use sticky tape to stick it together permanently. DO NOT TAPE THE TOP OF THE BOX AS THIS MUST BE ABLE TO OPEN AND CLOSE DURING THE EXPERIMENT. Your choice chamber is now complete and you can begin the next stage.

You will now need the water, pieces of stick (ice-lolly stick is ideal) and some woodlice. Collect the woodlice outside from under stones or beneath pieces of rotting wood. Keep them in the jar or tub until needed. Remove the rubber bands. If you look at your box you will see it has three different ends. These are the three chambers the woodlice can choose between and you should fill each of them in a different way. To begin with, try putting two or three dry sticks in each of chambers two and three. Soak the remaining sticks in water for five minutes before putting them in

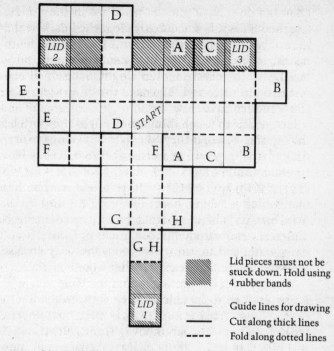

D

LID
2

A   C   LID
           3

E   B

E   D   START

F   F   A   C   B

G   H

G   H

LID
1

Lid pieces must not be
stuck down. Hold using
4 rubber bands

——— Guide lines for drawing

——— Cut along thick lines

- - - - Fold along dotted lines

Assembled choice chamber

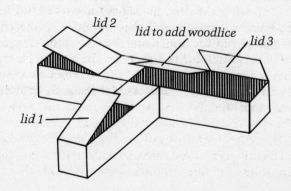

lid 2   lid to add woodlice   lid 3

lid 1

chamber one. Now put the woodlice in the middle (marked START) and quickly close the lids. Use the elastic bands to hold the lids shut but fold the lid of chamber three *up* so that light can enter that chamber. Leave the experiment in a light place for fifteen to thirty minutes and then open the lid to see where the woodlice have gone.

If they like to touch things in the light they will be in chamber three. If they like to touch things in dry, dark places they will be in chamber two. If they like to touch things in wet, dark places (which is what we expect them to like) they will be found in chamber one, which is where, hopefully, you will find them. You can try changing what is contained in each chamber using different foods, sticks or stones, light, dark, water and anything else you want to try. In that way you can find out exactly what woodlice like.

When you have finished experimenting you will know enough to be able to keep some woodlice as pets. All you need is a reasonably large container (a clear glass or plastic jar or bowl), some garden soil, a few pieces of tree bark, dead leaves, twigs and some water. The woodlice will live happily with all these things, but make sure the lid has a few small holes in it. This will let air into the container so that the woodlice can breathe. Keep the soil damp (but not wet) and remember to keep the container cool just as it is in the dark, damp cracks the woodlice choose to live in. Finally, don't forget to let them all go after a few months.

Did You Know

- Woodlice normally eat only dead leaves and other rotting plant material, but when there are too many woodlice and not enough food they will eat living plants.

- The shell plates of a woodlouse are made of a substance called chitin (*kite-in*). Chitin is the hardest substance known to be made by any living thing. It is even harder than tooth, bone or wood.

Slugs and Snails

What would you say was the most horrible type of animal in the world? There must be hundreds of different answers because everyone dislikes different things, but one thing most of us have in common is that we don't like slimy, wet animals. So when you pick up a stone in the garden or look under your favourite cabbage, it isn't surprising that the sight of a slug makes you feel like saying, 'yeuch!' So go out and find a slug and pick it up. (Always wet your hands with cold water before handling slugs and snails to prevent the heat from them burning the cold animals.) It really is revolting. It is cold and wet and leaves a trail of slime on your hand. It eats plants, especially green, juicy ones, including the vegetables gardeners grow for us to eat. How could anyone like a wet, cold, ugly animal that leaves slime wherever it goes and spends most of its life eating our food? Here we have a good example of a creepy-crawly.

So what is a slug? Well a good description would be to call it a naked snail. Slugs aren't worried about being naked – in fact, in some ways it has helped them, as they can slide into smaller spaces than snails. The similarity of slugs and snails is not an accident as they are closely related. Other close relations are many of the snail-like animals found on rocks or under the sand in the sea, such as winkles, mussels, oysters, scallops and clams. All of these have a shell but slugs aren't the only 'naked snails'. Others include cuttlefish, which hide their shells inside themselves (the shells are fed to budgerigars), squid and octopus. All are members of a group of animals called molluscs (*moll-lusks*) and they all have one thing in common. Believe it or not, their whole body is made of only two parts joined together – a head and a foot. No wonder people think slugs are ugly. What would you look like with just a head and foot?

The foot is used for movement and all molluscs can move. Slugs and snails are usually thought of as slow but octopus or squid can move very quickly. Even slugs can move quite quickly when they have a reason. Like all animals, including us, slugs are very fond of food but there is one type of food that they find almost impossible to resist. Beer! To see how fast a slug can move try getting one to follow a beer trail.

Get a sheet of glass or plastic and a small cup of beer. Dip your finger in the beer and draw a nice wet line across the glass with it. Then put the slug on one end of the line pointing towards the other end. If your line is not too wet you might see how fast a slug can really move.

The head of a mollusc not only drinks, it eats and allows the animal to see where it's going. Slugs and snails have small eyes on the end of eye stalks, which look a bit like tentacles, but although they look a bit strange they are good eyes and allow the creatures to see quite well. Octopus have enormous eyes, which are excellent at finding food and watching out for enemies.

Of course, apart from a head and foot some molluscs do have a few other bits. Many of them have shells which help protect them. For those that live in water the shell is usually quite thick and strong and protects the soft body from animals that might try to eat it. Although the shell is relatively heavy the water helps to lighten the load, so it doesn't really slow the animal down. For those that live on land the shell is usually thinner but still protects the soft body from attack. Much more important than this, the shell helps prevent the body drying out. By keeping the body wet the shell allows snails to move around in the sun which slugs do not dare do. If a slug is slow getting under a rock or into the shade it will die. A snail will just be a bit later getting its sleep.

No molluscs have bones. This means that slugs and snails are forced to remain small as they have no bones to support their bodies. In the sea there are no problems with support as the water does all the supporting needed. This means that some molluscs can grow very big as long as they live in the sea and these include octopus and squid. Octopus as big as humans live in the cold Pacific Ocean off the coast of Washington State, USA. Squid can be even bigger. Sucker marks on whales have led scientists to believe that the largest squid are 30 metres(100') long or more. That must make them the largest creepy-crawlies in the world.

How To Race Snails

You will need
- a piece of chalk
- some slugs or snails
- a glass jar or plastic tub
- a flat piece of pavement
- a little beer may help

What to do
Collect some slugs or snails from the garden or a field. Night-time is the best time to find them. If you have to search in the day, look underneath leaves or stones. Keep them in a glass or plastic container and make sure they are kept cool. Mark a small circle on the ground. This is where the race will start from. Now mark another circle around the small one so that the smaller one (the start line) is right in the middle of the big one. Don't make it too big or you'll never see the end of the race as the larger circle is the finish line. When each owner is ready to race his or her pet, put them all in the middle. Make sure somebody shouts 'go' and the big race is on. Whichever animal touches the outside circle first is the winner. You can decide if it is allowed to tempt them forward with some beer or not. Make sure you race only in the evening or on a cool, cloudy day as slugs and snails do not usually like sunlight.

How To See The Way Molluscs Move

You will need
   a small sheet of hard   a slug or large snail
     transparent plastic

What to do
Make sure your plastic is clean and dry. Wet your hands and pick up the slug or snail. Put it in the middle of the plastic sheet. When it begins to move, pick the plastic up and hold it vertically by its edge and watch the slug or snail from the other side. You will be looking at the animal's foot through the plastic. If you look very carefully you will see that the long edges of the foot seem to move in waves. It is this wave action that makes the body move forward.

Other animals can use body waves to move. Fish swim by moving their bodies from side to side in waves. We can also move using waves. Surfers can move by letting their bodies float on ocean waves, but that is cheating. Swimmers can actually make their own body waves to move. The body waves are not side to side like fish but up and down instead. This is called the butterfly stroke but as people aren't very good at making body waves, swimmers get some extra power by using their hands and arms. If you can swim why not find someone to teach you the butterfly stroke. Then you can try doing it without your arms and see how well you can use body waves to help you move.

Did You Know

- All snail shells coil in the same direction but nobody knows why.

- The largest shelled mollusc is the Giant Clam which has been measured at over 1.25m(4') and can live to be over one hundred years old.

- There are swimming snails! They all use their feet to swim. Some move the whole foot, while others have wing-shaped extensions that can flap. Sea butterflies flap their foot one hundred times each minute when swimming. Some sea butterflies, such as *Limacina* (*lie-mah-see-nah*) have shells. Others, including *Cymbulina* (*sim-bue-lee-nah*) have no shell. Sea hares are another type of swimming snail. *Aplysia punctata* (*ap-lie-see-ah punk-tah-tah*) flaps. *Aplysia saltator* (*ap-lie-see-ah sawl-tah-tor*) uses its foot to squeeze water quickly. This acts as a form of jet propulsion. Sea slugs, some of which have a shell, can also swim.

- Squid can swim at 55km per hour(35m per hour).

- The most dangerous snail is a Cone Shell. It has a dart which can inject a deadly poison into anything unlucky enough to come too near. It can kill a human, but fortunately this rarely happens. It lives in sand under the sea and is found in some tropical seas, particularly around Pacific islands such as Hawaii and Tahiti.

- Most molluscs use their tongues to eat their food. It is very rough, like a file, and is rubbed on food to break it into pieces the molluscs can swallow. The roughness is created by tiny teeth that cover the tongue. There may be 15,000 teeth on a mollusc's tongue.

🐉 Ladybirds

Once again we return to the world of insects to discover yet another type of creepy-crawly. When we looked at bluebottles, we saw that flies have unprotected wings. You may by now have discovered for yourself that flies can fold their wings back alongside their bodies, although each wing actually stays in its proper shape. Butterflies and moths have wings that they can move up or down but which cannot be folded back at all. They also have caterpillars that have false legs as well as six true legs. The ladybird is different again. It is an insect so it still has six true legs. It also has wings but they can be folded back along the body. They can also change shape so each separate wing can actually fold up, and finally the folded wings can be protected by a hard cover. We call this sort of insect a beetle.

Beetles are a wonderful group of animals that are of enormous interest, but of all the different beetles in the world one that people always find attractive is the ladybird. In general appearance it resembles other beetles. The body is round and slightly flattened and there are six legs with two very small feelers. Actually those feelers are really very important.

Although it has two good-sized eyes they aren't much use and the poor ladybird is nearly blind. It can't even see other ladybirds when it is almost touching them. The feelers are very sensitive to touch and vibration so they are used to find shelter, food and other ladybirds. You would expect feelers to be very large in nearly blind animals but in this case, strangely enough, they are tiny and almost impossible to see. Large feelers allow an insect to feel things from a distance. If you feel something and you think it is dangerous, the extra distance allows you a chance to get away before it's too late. After all, no one wants to turn up for dinner only to find out that they are the main course!

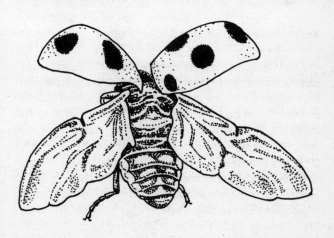

ladybird with hard wing covers raised and wings unfolded for flying

So why are ladybird feelers so short? Perhaps it is because the ladybird is very well protected. Ants, which often attack them, are incredibly strong but cannot break through the tough wing cases that completely cover their body. Other bigger animals that might fancy a light snack also avoid ladybirds. It isn't because they think they are too small or beautiful. The honest answer is that they taste awful (if you feel hungry don't try eating ladybirds). In case you forget, the pretty colours will remind you. In nature black and yellow (or black and red) are warning colours (something you will learn more about in the chapter on frogs and toads). Animals with those colours are always saying 'stay away!' because they are poisonous, dangerous or taste horrible. Therefore, well-protected animals such as the ladybird don't worry about being attacked, so they don't need long feelers. By the way, the real name for a feeler is antenna (an-ten-ah), and two feelers are antennae (an-ten-eye).

During the winter ladybirds hibernate, often looking for somewhere slightly sheltered such as a hollow in a tree or in between leaves. If they can find each other they even huddle together for a little warmth. In spring they wake up and find a mate, using the feelers to smell and touch. The female then lays eggs in small groups. The eggs are very tasty so they hope that any hungry animal that finds the eggs will not be hungry enough to eat them all. The yellow eggs turn black just before they hatch which takes about one week altogether. The baby ladybird or larva looks a lot like the adult but it is black and has no wings. It is also very hungry. Luckily for us they eat greenfly and blackfly, two pests that damage garden plants. Incidentally, they eat their food while it is still alive. Yeuch!

The larvae grow inside their hard skin, which eventually splits. This changing of skin is called moulting. The larvae do this three times and then turn into a pupa for a week. Inside the pupa case the larva grows wings. Very few other changes occur except, perhaps, the colour. (Read more about pupae in the chapter on caterpillars.) When the pupa case splits, out crawls the adult but without any spots. Only when the sun has dried the new skin do the lovely spots appear.

This is the third time so far in this book that we have learnt about insects changing shape as they become adults. Baby flies look like maggots, baby butterflies look like caterpillars, and now we know that baby ladybirds look like adult ladybirds with their wings missing. All baby insects start out looking at least slightly different from the adults. We know they will soon change shape and we call this process metamorphosis (*met-ah-more-foe-sis*). As you can see, this word is a bit of a mouthful but just to complicate things even more there are two different types of metamorphosis. The type we see with ladybirds and other beetles (as well as some other insects), where only a few small changes need to occur, is called incomplete metamorphosis. With the other type, enormous changes have to take place as the babies look nothing like the adult. This type is called complete metamorphosis.

How To Keep Ladybirds

You will need

a glass or plastic
   aquarium
some old net curtain
some greenflies or
   blackflies

a length of elastic
a pair of scissors
a few small house
   plants
some ladybirds

or

a cardboard box with
   top
a pencil
glue or sticky tape
some old net curtain
some greenflies or
   blackflies

some clear cellophane
a ruler
a pair of scissors
a few small house
   plants
some ladybirds

What to do

At the end of the winter make your 'cage'. Follow the
instructions for the caterpillar cage which can be
found in the chapter on caterpillars. If you use an
aquarium you only need to cut a piece of net and fit it
as a top, using the elastic to hold it in place. Alternatively you can make a cage from an old cardboard box.
The front must be clear, so use cellophane. The lid
must allow air to get in and out so cut a hole and cover
it with a piece of old net curtain which can be glued in
place. Of course, if you built a cage for the caterpillars
you can keep them, the greenflies and the ladybirds in
it at the same time.

   Put some soil in the cage, but if you used a box, put
a sheet of plastic inside so that the soil cannot touch
the bottom and sides of the box. Get a few small
indoor or house plants and plant them in the cage.
Try to use plants that have soft stems and leaves, not

cacti or others with hard leaves that the greenflies will dislike. Now find some greenflies or blackflies. That's really very easy. Any gardener will be very pleased to help you. Put the flies in your cage and hunt for some ladybirds (see below). When they are in the cage keep it in a bright place indoors but not where the sun can burn the plants. Water the soil whenever it is nearly dry and make sure the ladybirds always have a few greenflies or blackflies to eat.

If you are lucky, the ladybirds will lay eggs in the summer and you can watch them develop before winter. It might be fun for you to try and see each different stage in the life of a ladybird. Try to find the eggs, a baby without wings and an adult. Finally, don't forget to let all the animals go before the winter. You must do this before the weather gets too cold for them to be able to fly, as they will have to hunt for a place to hibernate for the winter.

Finding Different Types Of Ladybirds

You will need
- a small, clear glass or plastic bottle
- a magnifying glass is useful
- a small notebook
- a pen or pencil

What to do
Any time of the year except the cold season is suitable for looking for ladybirds. Look on plant stems and under leaves to find any. If you do find one, carefully put it in the bottle so that you can count its spots without it flying away. Immediately take a close look and count them. Record what you find in your notebook.

See how many different types of ladybird you can find. You can usually tell the difference between one species and another by the number of spots and what colour they are. Once again, let all the animals go as soon as you can, and be careful with them while you keep them.

A Simple Ladybird Experiment

You will need
   a ladybird on a leaf or branch

What to do
Begin this very easy experiment by gently tapping the plant on which the ladybird is resting. When the ladybird falls off, watch what it does. That's the whole experiment finished! I told you it was easy. The result should always be the same. It tucks in its legs even before it hits the ground and for a few seconds it plays dead, not moving at all. This is done just in case an animal is hungry and has forgotten what the warning colours mean. Most animals will

not eat a dead insect so the ladybird pretends to be dead. Don't worry though – you cannot hurt a ladybird by making it fall to the ground.

Did You Know

- There are over forty species of ladybird in Britain and about 4000 species in the world.

- One ladybird larva can eat as many as thirty to forty greenflies each day, which is a bit like you trying to eat fifty to sixty melons each day (except that I think the melons would taste nicer!).

Greenfly

Talk to any gardener about why some of their plants die and you can be sure there will be lots of reasons. They will tell you it was too hot or too cold, someone sold them a bad plant, slugs and snails ate it or someone trod on it. A gardener's life is certainly made difficult by the large number of animals that can attack and damage any plant. One that is found throughout the world is the greenfly.

Its proper name is aphid (*af-fid*), which is much better than greenfly because it can be green, brown, black or white. They are insects and so have six legs, and they have wings. They feed by sucking plant juices which is really where they become a problem. First of all they weaken and sometimes kill plants by sucking the goodness out of them. Secondly, because their mouths pierce the plant to suck out the juice, they are just as likely to put something into the plant as they are to suck out sap. This means they can accidentally give the plant diseases and in this way cause whole fields of food to die. Therefore the aphids are generally considered the worst enemy of the gardener and no one will speak very kindly of them.

However, they do have one protector. Aphids are

farmed by ants. Aphids produce tiny droplets of a sugar solution which they release every so often. Ants find this liquid irresistible and collect the juice as often as possible. To make sure of their supply they will often protect aphids from other animals and will even move them about. Presumably they move the aphids either to fresh bits of the plant or to somewhere the ant prefers, because it is nearer the ant's nest or it is safer. In other words, ants look after their aphids just as we look after cows. The aphids do not seem to be bothered by the ants at all and certainly don't try to resist them, or run or fly away. In fact, some scientists think that aphids may make the fluid just to attract ants, because ants protect them better than they can themselves.

Aphids do have some defences. Their major one is rather strange. If attacked they shake violently. You can see this for yourself if you try the simple experiment at the end of this chapter.

These curious little insects are unusual in the way they reproduce. Some of them produce new young that are absolutely identical to themselves and do this without mating. This method of producing young is called parthenogenesis (*path-en-oh-gen-eh-sis*) and is sometimes known as virgin birth. (You can read about this in other animals, such as bees and some microscopic pond animals, elsewhere in this book.) The young are born alive and look very much like the adults. Up to seven generations of aphid can be produced in this way, but then a new generation must be produced from female eggs that have been fertilized by a male. These eggs are used to make sure the animals survive during the winter.

Finally, there is one more interesting note on aphids. They are very fussy eaters. Each type has its own special plants, often only one or two, that it likes to eat. Aphids which prefer two different plants are usually very fussy about when they eat which one. For part of their life they will only eat one type of plant. Then, along with a change in the daylight and temperature, they will move on to another type of food. In other words, what they eat and where they live can depend on the season of the year.

Watching Greenfly Protect Themselves

You will need
    a small paint brush   a plant with greenfly
                                    on it

What to do
Go outside with your small paint brush and find a

plant with lots of greenfly on it. Very gently tickle one or two greenfly. Watch what happens.

What you should see is that the greenflies you tickle throw themselves wildly about, probably falling off the plant. If you look carefully you may also see other nearby greenflies wildly shaking about and falling off. This is a greenfly's way of protecting itself. The idea is that the wild movement so surprises other animals that they don't attack it, or the greenfly falls out of sight. Either way the greenfly would be safe. What a shame it doesn't often work. However, if you only tickled one or two greenfly, how did all the others know to go wild? The answer is that the ones you tickled told them by squirting some chemicals into the air. All insects send messages to each other using chemicals. They are called pheromones (*feromoans*). They are particularly powerful in moths and butterflies as you can read elsewhere in this book.

Did You Know

- When ants take the sugary solution from greenfly it is called 'milking'.

- Greenfly have absolutely no defence against lacewing larvae which love to eat them. If a lacewing larva attacks them they do nothing. They seem to just wait to be eaten, as if they have given up.

7 Worms

Some animals really are not very popular. In some cases there are very good reasons (they may be dangerous, for example), but some creatures have to suffer very bad reputations simply because people don't like them enough to find out the truth about them. One such animal is the spider and you can learn how misunderstood they were if you read about the tarantula further on in the book. Another creepy-crawly has really had to suffer. The worm's reputation was damaged by the fact that centuries ago snakes were also referred to as worms by many people, among them no less a person than William Shakespeare, the great English poet and playwright. This obviously encouraged people to believe worms were dangerous. Lots of people also called maggots 'worms' and as there aren't many people who like maggots, again the poor worms had to suffer being thought of as ugly and dirty. As we now know, snakes and maggots are not worms. Real worms are very different and come in all shapes and sizes. Some are even amazingly beautiful as you will learn.

You may be surprised to discover that there are many different types of worm. The most important

tube-worm

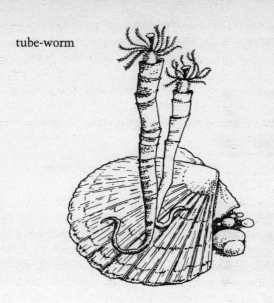

earthworm

leech

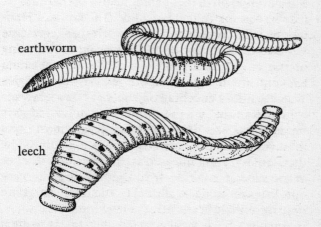

Three types of worm

are true worms, but there are a lot of worm-like animals that have been called worms. True worms, like the common earthworm found in most gardens, can easily be identified by rings which mark the body. There are in fact about 9000 different kinds or species of true worms.

Here is a list of the animals most popularly known as worms:

hairworms	roundworms
flatworms	threadworms
ribbon worms	bristle worms
earthworms	leeches
spiny-headed worms	peanut worms
spoon worms	arrow worms
tufted tube-worms	bearded worms
sausage-shaped worms	acorn worms

The best known of these are the earthworms but you may have seen or heard of a few of the others. Hairworms, flatworms and roundworms are not true worms and their bodies therefore do not have ring markings. (If you would like to read about them you can find them in the chapter called 'Microscopic Water Animals & other Pond Creepy-Crawlies'.)

Bristle and tufted tube-worms are almost always found in the sea. The bristle worms are most commonly seen by people whose hobby is fishing. The ragworm is commonly used as bait and can be dug out of the sand at low tide. If you get the chance to see one, keep your fingers clear of its mouth. It can give a nasty bite. A close relative, the lugworm, is harmless. It also lives in wet sand or mud but if you try to dig it up you have to hurry. A lugworm can dig a burrow more quickly than most people can dig it up. Tube-worms are probably the prettiest worms of all. They live in the sea and attach themselves to rocks or dig into the sand. Then around them they build a tube of sand, mud or shells which they stick together. Although the tube is usually fairly dull, the worm is not. It lives almost entirely within the tube but sticks its head out to feed. The head is surrounded by tentacles that wave in the air and catch any tiny particles in the water. These tiny, often microscopic, living particles are called plankton and are eaten by the worm. The tentacles look like a beautiful fan and can be brightly coloured. It is well worth trying to see one. They are usually found in the aquarium at zoos, or a pet shop that sells live marine fish may have some.

Leeches are known to most people. They are always found in or near water, most of them in freshwater ponds or rivers. The exceptions are tropical leeches, some of which live in very damp forests, and a very few marine leeches (which live in the sea). Most of these horrifying creatures live by sucking blood from other animals. Many of them feed off animals like frogs, snails, birds or fish. A few will feed from us. They use a sucker at each end of the body to move in 'loops' and some can swim well. Although most leeches are only a few centimetres in length they can be as long as 30cm(1').

Everyone has seen an earthworm. They are long and thin and look as if they are wet – a perfect description of a creepy-crawly. They live in the top few inches of the soil, usually coming to the surface in very wet weather or at night. In the winter they dig deeper into the ground and will often group together to keep warm.

Earthworms eat almost any dead bits of plant or animal that will fit into their small mouths. They also drag bigger bits of plants from the ground surface down into their burrows. They may chew these big pieces but generally they eat by swallowing soil. Any bits of food in the soil are digested in their gut. All the indigestible soil goes straight through and out the other end as waste. The waste is left on the surface of the soil at night in coiled mounds called castings. Although they eat most things they are, in fact, quite fussy eaters. They prefer particular types of food and it does depend on whether the food is very fresh (live but beginning to die) or dead. Here is an earthworm menu showing what they like:

An Earthworm Menu

	Live Leaves	Dead Leaves
Best Food	Beech	Willow
	Maple	Oak
	Oak	Lime
	Horse Chestnut	Beech
	Lime	Maple
Worst Food	Willow	Horse Chestnut

When earthworms begin to reproduce they can be found lying next to each other, head to tail. They don't have to search hard for each other as any other earthworm will do. This is because all earthworms are male and female at the same time. This is called hermaphrodite (*her-maff-roe-dite*).

How To Hunt Worms

You will need
- a torch
- a jar
- rubber gloves
- some transparent red cellophane
- sticky tape or a rubber band

What to do
Begin this very simple little exercise by covering the end of your torch with the red cellophane. Use the sticky tape or rubber band to hold it on. Now wait until dark and then go out hunting for worms with a jar and the torch. Wear the rubber gloves so that any worms you touch are not burnt by your hot hands. We are warm-blooded but they are cold-blooded and easily burnt. Tread very, very softly as worms can feel the slightest vibrations. Worms cannot see red light so you will be able to creep up to them and quickly grab them before they go back into their burrows.

How To Make A Wormery

You will need
- two 30cm × 30cm pieces of clear perspex or glass
- two 30cm × 2.5cm × 2.5cm pieces of wood (smooth finish)
- silicone rubber glue
- ordinary garden soil
- sieved soil
- leaves
- chalky soil
- sticky tape
- one piece of 25cm × 2.5cm × 2.5cm wood
- two pieces of 15cm × 2.5cm × 2.5cm wood
- sand
- peat
- black paper
- worms

What to do

Place one sheet of perspex on a table. (You can use glass but perspex is much safer.) Take the two longest pieces of wood and stick them along two opposite

completed wormery

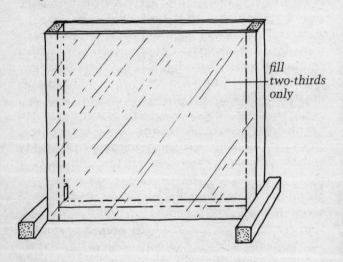

fill two-thirds only

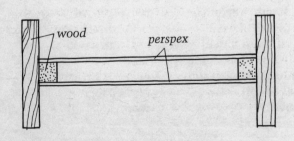

wood

perspex

edges of the plastic using the silicone rubber glue. The slightly shorter piece should now fit along the bottom edge of the perspex between the first two pieces of wood. Stick it there and make sure you use glue wherever wood touches wood. Now stick the other sheet on top of the wood to make a box with one open end. Use sticky tape to hold everything together and leave the box for twenty-four hours so the glue can harden. Stand the box up with the open end at the top. Stick one short piece of wood at the bottom on each side to make a stand. Leave this for another twenty-four hours. The wormery is now built and should be able to stand up unsupported. Now fill it with layers of different soils. Make each layer 3cm(1") deep and put layers of different colours on top of each other. You can use garden soil, sieved soil, peat, sand and chalky soil. If you can get any you can try different coloured sands instead of some of the other soils. Finally tear up leaves into small pieces and put these on the top layer. Now put two or three worms (no more) in the wormery. Cover both sides with black paper so light cannot get in. Put the wormery somewhere not too hot and fairly dull. Keep the soil slightly damp all the time.

From time to time you can look in your wormery by removing a piece of black paper. You should be able to see the worm burrows, worm castings, the worms living in their burrows and how they quickly mix up all the soil. When the soil is well mixed tip out all the soil and worms and start again. Use fresh worms which you should handle with rubber gloves or wet hands. Remember to put worms back on to soil at night or to cover them gently with some loose soil.

What Food Do Worms Like?

You will need

    a wormery   2 or 3 worms
    different sorts of food

What to do

Put soil and worms into the wormery. Remember to keep the soil slightly damp at all times. Now find some different types of food. Try different kinds of live and dead leaves or bits of fruit or different kinds of raw vegetables. Chop them up so they are small enough for the worms to eat. Then put some of them into the wormery, each in a different pile. See which foods the earthworms like best. Perhaps you might like to see if the earthworm menu you've read about is really true.

Did You Know

- One acre of land may contain well over one thousand million worms.

- Australian giant earthworms can be 3.96m(13') long.

- Worms in South Africa usually weigh much less than Australian worms but they can be longer, the largest measured being 6.7m(22') long.

- Bearded worms live at the bottom of the ocean 10,000m(30,000') below the surface.

- Leeches were often used in the past to cure people of illnesses. Diseases were thought to be caused by poisoned blood so medicinal leeches were put on the body to suck out the poison. (Yeuch!) This became very unpopular (except in Italy) until very recently. Now medicinal leeches are being used again by doctors. Their mouths produce a substance that prevents blood from going hard (or clotting) which is useful in some patients whose blood may clot dangerously.

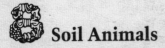 **Soil Animals**

Have you ever wondered just how many types of animal live all about you or how many animals there are under every leaf or stone? We live in an amazing world. Almost every part of our planet is home to some creature or other, from the depths of the deepest ocean to near the top of the highest mountains, and from the edges of the Arctic and Antarctic ice caps to the centre of the great deserts. But we are usually totally unaware of these animals. The reason is simple. Almost all the animals in the world are tiny, many of them being so small that you can only see them with the help of a microscope.

Many such small animals live in soil. They include worms, spiders, scorpion-like animals (pseudoscorpions), beetles, mites (tiny relatives of the spider), leatherjackets (caterpillar-like larvae that grow into daddy-long-legs), millipedes, centipedes, slugs, snails, weevils and woodlice. They may be small but soil animals are important for many different reasons. First of all they provide food for bigger animals. For example, the smallest insects living in the soil can be eaten by larger insects. These can in turn be eaten by frogs and frogs can be eaten by

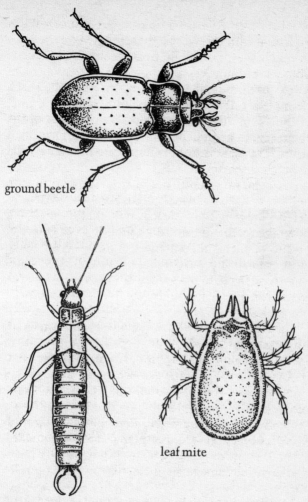

ground beetle

earwig

leaf mite

Some soil animals. The earwig and ground beetle are
insects, whereas the mite is related to the spider

people. Frogs' legs are a delicacy in France, and in Martinique (in the West Indies) people like the taste so much they call edible frogs 'mountain chicken'. There are countless examples of this process in which each animal is eaten by a larger one. Each example is called a food chain. If the smallest animal in the chain died, all the animals in the rest of the chain would be in danger of dying as well, so small animals in the soil are very important for the survival of much larger animals.

A second function that soil animals perform is in helping to keep the world clean. Have you ever wondered what happens to dead leaves, dead animals and other things that lie on the ground? If it isn't made of plastic or metal the smallest animals will help to clear it up. They eat the bits of rubbish that would otherwise make the countryside look a mess, including all the dead leaves and animals as well as some of our rubbish.

Yet a third reason why the smallest soil animals are important is that some of them can be pests and, instead of helping us, do a lot of harm. There are two main types of pest. Some damage our food and others cause disease. Weevils are only about 3mm(⅛″) long, often smaller, and yet only one needs to get into a store of grain and the whole store may be destroyed. Weevils breed very quickly and eat very quickly. Once they have infected a store they usually breed and do their damage before anyone notices they are there.

Many other animals are pests in the same way. Of the disease carriers there are again many to choose from. A variety of tiny worms cause all sorts of problems, especially where people live with their farm animals or where medicines are difficult to get. Some can even dig holes in skin and then crawl inside to begin a tour of the body. It's wonderful for them but not much fun for the unlucky person. Fortunately these nasty worms don't live everywhere but are usually found only in some tropical countries. If you live in such a country you have to know how to avoid catching these worms.

Other disease-carrying pests are less fussy about where they live. Fleas are found everywhere and feed off blood which they suck, like vampires, from their victims. They can carry several diseases but perhaps the most famous is the Bubonic Plague. In the seventeenth century this killer disease spread all the way from Africa, throughout Europe and into Britain. Luckily, the Great Fire of London helped to kill off the fleas and the disease is not found in Britain any more and is quite rare elsewhere.

So, now that you know that the soil can contain millions of creatures of all shapes and sizes, perhaps you would like to have a look at some. Don't be worried about the animals. Providing you follow the instructions below you will not be attacked!

The Funnel Experiment

You will need

a very large funnel

a jam jar, small tin can or tub

a magnifying glass or microscope, if available

a paper or plastic bag

some damp, dead leaves

a table lamp if available

	with
a large metal can with the lid	a drill and bit

	or
a large plastic tub with the lid	a knife

What to do

Collect together everything you need *except the leaves*. Make a hole in the middle of the large metal or plastic lid. This is not as easy as it looks so ASK AN ADULT TO HELP YOU DO THIS. If the lid is made of plastic, the hole can be cut out with a knife. If you have a metal lid you will need to use a drill and bit. In either case the hole must be large enough to allow the neck of the funnel to fit it. When the lid is put on the container the funnel should be supported above it so the neck empties into the middle.

Put the jam jar, small tin or tub inside the large can or tub so it is in the middle. Put the lid on the large container and put the funnel neck in the hole. Now collect some damp leaves, dead and rotting from the ground, and put them quickly in your bag. You should try to get a nice handful all in one go so that any creepy-crawlies aren't frightened away before you get them in the bag. Put the leaves in the top of the funnel and wait. If you managed to get a table lamp you can shine it on to the top leaves from about 15 cm (6″) away.

After about thirty minutes animals will begin to collect in the jam jar. The leaves in the funnel will be drying, especially if the light is near them, and most creepy-crawlies do not like to be too dry. The leaves at the top dry first so the animals move down to stay in the dampness which we already know, from the choice-chamber experiment with woodlice, many creepy-crawlies like. As they go down they get into the slippery funnel neck and eventually fall down into the jar. Now there is a problem. Some of the

The funnel experiment

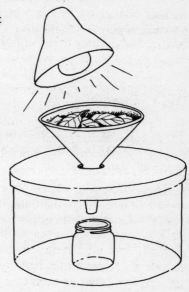

animals you collect will be harmless, living on dead or dying bits of plants, but others are hunters and will gladly kill and then eat any animal small enough to catch. So, if you leave it too long before looking in the jam jar, all you will find will be the hunters. If you want to see all the animals you collected with the leaves, you will have to stay and watch what happens.

If you want to look more closely at your animals you can tip them out on to a piece of white paper. A magnifying glass will help you see them in more detail. If you can get hold of a microscope, it will also allow you to see much more detail. (Hobby shops usually sell small microscopes at very reasonable prices.) Try sorting them out into insects (those with six legs) and others. You may very well be surprised at how many animals there are and what they look like. With animals like these you don't need Martians. They all look as if they could be from another planet.

Did You Know

- 1 acre (4,840 square yards) of land may be home to as many as 100,000,000 insects. Most of them are found in or on the soil.

- There are more than 850,000 different kinds of insect, which is more than three times the number of all the other animals in the world.

- Almost all the animals that live between the wood of a tree and the bark are insects.

Water Insects and their Relatives

If you took all the animals in a pond and weighed them, which type do you think would weigh most? Yes, you probably guessed correctly. The answer is the insects and their relatives weigh more than all the other animals put together. In fact, not only do they weigh more, but there is also a greater number of different types than all the others put together. In other words, there are an awful lot of insects and their relatives, which we call arthropods (*are-throw-pods*). In all there are nearly one million different kinds, and many of them live in water.

Arthropods include spiders, crustaceans and insects. These are probably the most interesting pond animals simply because there are so many different types and they are mostly big enough to see easily. Spiders are described later in the book, but you might like to know that one spider actually lives underwater and uses its web to hold a bubble of air from which it breathes. There are also fishing spiders that literally fish for their dinner, and a few other types that run around on the water plants, and occasionally on the water, looking for small insects.

Crustaceans are animals such as crabs, lobsters and

shrimps, all of which have ten legs. The easiest to see in a pond is probably the water flea or *Daphnia* (*daf-nee-ah*). It eats algae which it collects by using its front legs as filters, which then pass the food to the mouth. It doesn't use its legs to swim, surprisingly. Instead its antennae, which are very large, are used to create an upward jerk. To go down the water flea just stops swimming and sinks. The shell is completely transparent. Water fleas are fed to pet fish by their keepers and can easily be purchased in pet shops. The water louse is another common crustacean and is related to the land-living wood louse. It may be slightly bigger than the wood louse but does not grow beyond 25mm(1″). Like its relative it carries its eggs, which can be found underneath the body near the head. Water lice eat plants, particularly those that are dead or dying. For this reason they like smelly ponds.

Insects, you may recall, are animals with six legs. There are many, but few can be as attractive as the dragonfly. The name sounds fierce and is very suitable as both the beautiful adult and the rather ugly baby are very dangerous to anything that looks like food. A dragonfly will catch other insects while they are flying. It will grab the victim with its legs and then tear it to bits with its mouth. The baby or nymph (*nimf*) is just as fierce. It will eat almost any other animal, including other dragonfly nymphs and fish, and can certainly catch and kill any animal its own size. Damselflies are very similar to dragonflies, though often smaller. The nymphs are easy to identify as their tails end with three feather or leaf-like organs. These are gills used for breathing. Nymphs can take up to three years to turn into adults. When they are ready to change, usually at night, they climb

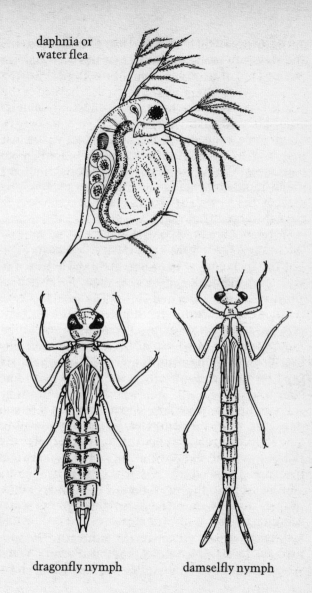

daphnia or
water flea

dragonfly nymph   damselfly nymph

out of the water on to a plant. Then the old skin splits and out crawls the beautiful adult. The wings are pumped full of blood and a few minutes later it can fly off in search of food and a mate.

Mayfly nymphs look very similar to, but smaller than, damselfly nymphs. They often have more gills. Mayfly adults are small and have short wide wings that look like lace. After the adult hatches it waits one day and then it sheds its skin and comes out as a much more colourful adult. Mayflies are the only insects that shed their skin as adults as well as when they are nymphs.

Water measurers are long, thin insects that walk on the water. They usually eat drowning insects but can kill small creatures. The long thin mouth is used to stab food and suck the goodness out. Pond skaters also live on the water and are very similar, but have smaller bodies with much longer legs. The middle legs are used to row across the water so each pair moves together just like oars in a rowing boat. The back legs steer the pond skater. The front legs are used for holding food after it has been caught and stabbed.

If you imagine an upside-down pond skater which lives just under the surface of the water, you will be able to recognize a water boatman. It is very like the skater even in the way it eats. The underwater measurer is called a water scorpion. It has a very similar shape to the measurer but its arms are better adapted to hold on to food. Another type of water scorpion looks less like the measurer as it is short and fat instead of being long and thin. Its arms are still just as deadly. Measurers, skaters, boatmen and water scorpions are all called bugs. All bugs have mouths that stick into their food and suck it out as a liquid. I suppose you could call bugs the vampires of the pond world.

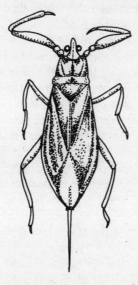

water boatman

Beetles are common in ponds but very few of the thousands of different types of beetle can actually live underwater. The diving beetles are probably the most fearsome, eating almost anything including fish bigger than themselves. They can be as big as 38mm(1½") so only birds and larger adult fish are totally safe from them in the pond. The larva is just as dangerous and in two years can grow as long as 5cm before it changes into an adult. Despite living in pond water diving beetles are very strong fliers and can easily move on to a new pond. Another common water beetle is the whirligig. These crazy little creatures, less than 22mm(⅞"), swim in little circles on the surface of the water, eating any drowning insects they find. If frightened the whirligig dives down and hangs on to something underwater for a while. It takes its own supply of air down with it, carrying some at its tail and some more under the wing cases.

Many flies grow up in water. The most well known is the dreaded mosquito. It is dreaded because it is not only a painful pest, but it also can carry dangerous and often deadly diseases. The life of a mosquito starts as an egg floating on water in a raft, although some mosquitoes let the eggs float by themselves. The egg hatches into a larva that spends much of its time hanging upside down below the water surface. It has a small tube, the siphon, that sticks out of the water to breathe in air. Food consists of any of the microscopic animals and plants in the water. A frightened larva dives by wriggling madly. When the wriggling stops the larva floats back up. The larva becomes a pupa which spends its life hanging head up below the water. It also has breathing tubes that allow it to breathe air. Eventually the pupa hatches into the adult.

The male must mate with a female before eggs can be produced. The males do little except live off nectar from flowers. The females must actually lay the eggs which is a major effort, and they need extra energy to fill the eggs with food. The female gets all this energy by feeding on blood. Unlike many animals that feed on blood, the mosquito isn't particular about which blood. She will happily drink from frogs, furred animals and, of course, you! To drink the blood she first pierces the skin and spits into the wound. Her spit stops the blood from hardening while she sucks it up. It is the spit that is dangerous. In tropical countries it can carry diseases such as malaria, yellow fever and the less well-known dengue (*den-ghee*) fever. Dengue fever is less serious as, unlike the other two diseases, it rarely kills. It makes you feel very tired for weeks or sometimes months and it can take a year for someone to fully recover. Fortunately, in cooler climates the mosquito doesn't cause disease, although the bite still creates a terrible itch, and the very high-pitched buzz of a mosquito can be just as annoying.

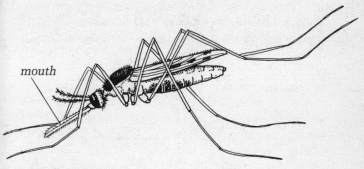

mouth

female mosquito

The caddis fly has a larva that is one of the most entertaining of all the creepy-crawlies in a pond. It looks a bit like a long thin beetle but you will not often see more than the head. It spends its life finding small bits and pieces and gluing them into a long, thin tube. The larva lives inside the tube and drags its home along wherever it goes. It is a very busy little animal, almost always moving, and therefore very

interesting and great fun to watch. The tubes are very
delicate and as they can be made of anything they can
be very beautiful. A collection of caddis fly larva
homes might be quite interesting. The adult is a
relation of butterflies and moths, the main difference
being that caddis fly wings are hairy.

Obviously there are hundreds of different experiments you could do with these animals, and you
could try to keep any of them in an aquarium or build
a pond for them. Perhaps most unusual of all would
be to try and watch them underneath the water in
their own ponds.

How To Build An Underwater Scope

You will need

a 30cm(12″) length of 10cm wide plastic tube	some transparent kitchen wrap
	a strong rubber band

or

a 30cm(12″) length of 10cm wide plastic tube	a file
	some silicone rubber glue
3mm thick transparent perspex	a hacksaw

What to do

For this exercise you can use plastic drainpipe which
is fairly easy to obtain. If you prefer you can use a tube
with a bigger diameter. It should be about 30cm(12″)
in length.

Now decide if you want a cheap and quick-to-make
scope, or one that will last a lot longer. The cheap
model can be made very quickly. Tear off a piece of

transparent kitchen wrap which should be the kind that clings to almost anything it touches. Stretch it gently over one end of the tube as if you were making a drum, and press the edges on to the side of the tube. Now put the rubber band around the plastic wrap and tube about 2cm(¾") from the sealed end. The cheap model is now finished.

Two underwater scopes

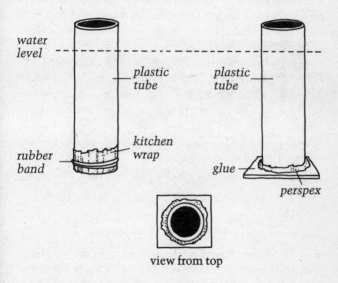

water level

plastic tube

plastic tube

kitchen wrap

rubber band

glue

perspex

view from top

The stronger model will need some 3mm(⅛") transparent perspex which you will probably be able to get from DIY (do-it-yourself) shops or any shop that sells plastic and glass. You will need a square piece that will just cover the end of your tube without leaving any holes or gaps. If the shop will cut it to shape for you, show them the tube. Squeeze some glue around one end of the tube so there are no gaps. Stick the transparent plastic sheet over the end of the tube. Leave it for at least twenty-four hours. Then, if you need to, gently cut and file any pieces of the sheet that are sticking out. Make sure an adult helps you do this as hacksaws and files can be dangerous. The scope is now ready.

To use your underwater scope you must find a pond. Push the scope into the water so you can look down the tube. The open end of the tube should be nearest to your eye and must stay above the water. You will find that by looking down the tube you will clearly see under the water. Without the tube, small ripples and reflections on the surface of the water make it very difficult to see more than vague outlines and shadows. You can now spy on the creepy-crawly life of your local ponds. Be careful when you use the scope. If you are going to hang over the water make sure someone is with you to stop you from falling in.

Did You Know

- The fishing spider dips the tips of some of its legs into the water to feel when a fish (or other type of food) touches the water surface nearby. When it feels a vibration the spider runs on top of the water and attacks the fish, grabbing and poisoning it. Just in case of accidents it uses a silk safety line to attach itself to land or a floating plant. It can actually attract fish by tapping the water with its legs, hoping a fish will come to investigate.

74

- Although water boatmen have piercing and sucking mouthparts like other bugs, they do not always eat animals. They suck sap from plants which is their preferred food. Other bugs usually eat animals.

- The largest insect the world has ever known was a prehistoric dragonfly.

Frogs and toads

Here are yet more examples of perfectly disgusting animals. Wet and slimy to look at, often an ugly greenish-brown colour and making a hideous, wet plop when they jump, you wouldn't think anything could be worse. And watching them eat is absolutely revolting, not just because they eat other horrible creepy-crawlies but because of the way they chew them, noisily enjoying every juicy crunch! Frogs and toads are found wherever there is dampness or fresh water, as long as the temperature is not too cold. Surprisingly there are also some that live in deserts by burrowing under the surface of the ground to find damp sand. Frogs and toads can vary in size from some that are about as big as your thumbnail to the enormous Goliath and bullfrogs that are as big as large grapefruits, but all of them are still easy to consider creepy-crawlies.

Of course, some people find frogs and toads beautiful, and if you do take the trouble to look at some of the unusual species you can see why. Many of the tree frogs found in tropical countries come in fantastic colours, varying from a plain but brilliant lime green to a dramatic mixture of black and red.

76

Although we find the colours pretty, they are far more important than might at first appear. In a jungle full of hungry animals a little frog would make a lovely mouth-sized snack. Very tasty if you're a lizard or a snake. As most of the leaves in the jungle are green, a very easy way to hide is to try to look like a leaf, so many tree frogs use a green skin colour to camouflage themselves. At the other extreme however, you will realize that black and red frogs can be seen on leaves very easily. Obviously these frogs don't mind being seen and there is a good reason. Black and red frogs taste disgusting as they are poisonous. The colour is used as a warning so that animals learn never to eat them. A hungry young snake may eat a black and red tree frog once, but it will soon spit it out. That frog might die but the snake will never eat another black and red frog again, so many others will live thanks to just one. Black and red are often used together in nature as warning colours, so remember – never try to eat a black and red frog.

Many frogs and toads use their throat and mouth to make a remarkable song. Although called a croak, the song can be pleasant to hear and watching the mouth while a frog croaks can be entertaining. To female frogs the song must be delightful because males use it to attract the females just before mating. If it didn't work there wouldn't be any tadpoles, so obviously the songs are a great success.

The Midwife Toad lays eggs which the male wraps around his ankles. He walks around like this, looking after the eggs, until they are ready to hatch. He then returns to water so the tadpoles can swim away. The Surinam Toad has to be one of the most remarkable of all. After the eggs are laid the male pushes them into the skin on the female's back. There small pouches form about them, enabling the mother to look after them until they hatch out, not as tadpoles but as baby toads. It is amazing to see baby toads hatch out of the mother's back and hop away to live their own lives.

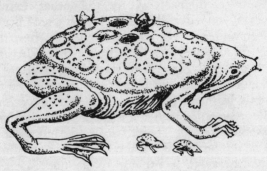

surinam toad with babies hatching out of pouches in its back

Frogs and toads are amphibians which means they have to return to water to reproduce. (You can learn more about the life cycle of frogs in the experiment 'How to keep frogs'.) Their soft skin is used to help the animals breathe but it must be wet if air is to be able to pass through it. So although they live on land, water must never be far away and they must also avoid the sun. In frogs the skin is usually smooth whereas toads have a rougher skin which we describe as warty. You can use this to tell one from the other. Another way of telling the two apart is to look at the slimy eggs. Frog eggs are layed in a mass with no particular shape. Toad eggs are layed in a string.

Only a few years ago frogs and toads were common in the countryside. Now in Britain they are very rare. In the 1970s they were so rare that many people thought they might die out altogether. Luckily groups were formed to protect these harmless creatures and now their numbers are increasing. You can even find signposts warning car drivers to be careful of frogs crossing the road, so that breeding frogs aren't run over as they try to get to ponds. There were several reasons why they were threatened. Ponds used to be very common in Britain, but as people built houses, ponds were filled in. If you destroy ponds, frogs have nowhere to breed, so they die out. Another reason was that teachers used to catch frogs to show in schools, often killing them (although they tried to do this painlessly). So many were caught that they became too rare to find. Luckily, when they realized what was happening, teachers stopped hunting frogs. Many also helped protect the remaining frogs and still do.

How To Keep Frogs

You will need

some frogs' eggs	a jar or plastic bag
a net	a fish tank
pond weed (*Elodea*)	water
some frog food (ants, worms or maggots)	rocks

What to do

Begin early in spring when the eggs will be found in ponds. Eggs are usually found in shallow water, near the edge of ponds or close to water plants, especially reeds. They often float and look like bubbles of jelly.

ASK PERMISSION OF THE POND OWNER
before taking any eggs. This is *very* important as frogs
in Britain are protected in the wild. You cannot
collect frogs' eggs, called frog spawn, from some
ponds. In some areas conservation groups exist and
they will be delighted to help you get some eggs if you
have a pond or are willing to help them. You will need
about twenty or more but don't take too many or they
will all die, as they need a lot of fresh, clean water to
stay healthy. Take a jar or plastic bag that is large
enough to hold the eggs and some water. When you
get home tip all the eggs and water into a fish tank. It
will help if the tank contains some Canadian pond
weed (*Elodea*) to add oxygen to the water. You can get
this from most pet shops.

You can now watch the eggs develop. Both frogs'
and toads' eggs develop in very much the same way,
but frogs lay their eggs in one big mass while toads lay
theirs in long strings. Each egg consists of a dark
centre covered in a transparent jelly. The jelly helps
to stop animals eating the tadpole. At first the dark
centre consists of a single cell but it quickly divides
into two. Then each half divides into two again. This
happens many times until a ball of cells is formed.
From that time it is difficult to see how each change
occurs but shortly a tadpole with an obvious head and
tail can be seen, looking very much like a fish. When
the tadpole is fully formed it wriggles free of the
remaining jelly.

Now you really will need some water plants such
as *Elodea*. They are a perfect place for algae to grow.
These are tiny or microscopic plants on which the
tadpoles feed. You must keep the tadpoles separate
because at this stage they will be eaten by fish, pond

animals and even other frogs. The tadpoles will not change (except in size) for a while and the only visible features are eyes, a mouth and gills. The gills allow the tadpole to breathe by absorbing oxygen from the water.

Very soon the tadpoles will want to eat meat. In the wild they eat tiny animals or pick at dead animals. Feed them a small piece of raw, red meat hung in the water on a piece of cotton so it can easily be fished out. If the tadpoles don't eat it then try again another day with fresh meat. Never leave meat in the water for more than a day. The first change you will notice in the shape of your tadpoles will be when the gills begin to disappear. They will start to move inside the body like those of a fish.

As they continue to grow you will be able to watch the legs form. First the back legs and then the front ones push their way out of the body. At the same time the gills and tail get smaller and smaller until eventually there is a perfectly formed but tiny frog or toad. Make sure there are some rocks in the water so that the frogs or toads can climb out if they want. At this stage you should let the baby frogs go. Put them back into a pond (near the edge). Only keep a very few frogs if you have a large tank with lots of dry soil for the frogs to live on and enough water for them to swim in. Your fish tank will need to be at least 1m(3') long and 48cm(18") deep. Feeding them at this stage is more difficult. They need ants and other live food of a similar size. When they get bigger they can take meal worms (obtained from pet shops), earthworms or almost any insect that will fit into their mouths. However, when you have seen the tadpoles change into baby frogs, the best thing to do is put the babies back in either the original pond or another one with clear water and plenty of healthy plants in it. You could even build a new pond in your garden (or a friend's) and put your frogs there.

Whichever you do you will increase the number of frogs in the wild and help them survive. Helping animals survive is called conservation and is an important thing for us to do. We need other plants and animals in the world. Sometimes we know why and other times we do not. But wouldn't the world be a bit more boring if all the frogs, toads and other similar animals suddenly disappeared for ever?

How To Build A Pond

You will need

a spade	some paving or
sand	stepping stones
a plastic pond liner	a garden hose
pond weed (*Elodea*)	other pond plants

What to do

Wherever you want to build a pond, make absolutely certain that, *before you begin*, you have permission to do so. Accidents can easily happen to people or property, so take the utmost care, and make sure that an adult supervises every stage of the pond's construction. Use the hose (it should not be attached to a tap) to mark out where the pond will be and what shape you want it. You can use string instead if the hose is too short. A big pond is easier to look after and will probably look prettier. It will also become a home to more animals. Remember, though, that the

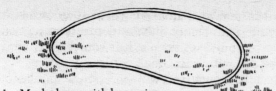

1   Mark shape with hose-pipe

2   Dig hole with step in it

3   Cover hole with pond liner and position by slowly
    filling with water

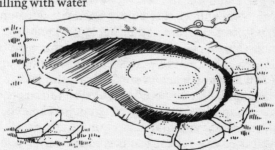

4   Trim excess liner and place paving stones around edge
    of pond

bigger the pond the more it will cost to build. A minimum area of four square metres (two metres long and two metres wide if it is square) is recommended and will fit into most gardens. Smaller sizes may become cloudy.

When the shape and position of the pond have been decided use the spade to dig out a shallow hole inside the outline marked by the hose. Do not dig deep yet. Remove the hose. Now, leave an outline or margin about 30cm(1′) wide and then dig out the area inside to a depth of about 24cm(9½″). The sides should slope slightly inwards. Now leave another margin of 30cm and then dig down to a further depth of between 24 and 75cm(9½″ to 2½′), again making sure the sides slope slightly inwards. Remove any obvious stones and then put a layer of sand, 3cm (1″) deep, on all the flat surfaces. Now cover the hole with the pond liner, attach the hose pipe to a tap, and use the water to help position the liner exactly. You do this by slowly filling the pond, and as the liner fits in help the liner fold wherever it needs to. Finally, fold the edges of the liner on to the top edge (with a layer of sand underneath it) and cover them with stepping stones. It is best to use 60cm(2′) wide stones as you can then let about 6cm(2½″) hang over the pond. This stops cats from easily catching the pond animals.

You are now ready to stock your pond. In the first week, only plants should be added as various chemicals in tap water might harm animals. Then you can add anything you like, but if you do add any fish do ask for advice. Good water garden centres and the better pet shops will tell you what plants and fish you should buy if you tell them how big your pond is and how much you want to spend. Names of recommended suppliers for everything to do with garden ponds are listed at the back of the book. Most of the creepy-crawlies found in ponds will arrive by themselves but if you want to speed things up it is quite easy. Simply find a local pond and collect a little of the mud and water. Pour this into your own pond and animals hidden in the mud will make your pond their new home. A few fish will be very attractive. Frogs, toads and newts are great fun and will eat slugs which damage garden plants. You can read more about slugs and newts elsewhere in the book.

Did You Know

- Frogs shut their eyes while they swallow food.

- Frogs have fallen from the sky like rain. Nobody knows how or why.

- One of the strongest poisons in the world is made from frogs. It is used by Amazonian Indians to paint the tips of arrows so that they always kill if they hit their target.

- Most frogs talk by croaking but there is one frog that talks by showing other frogs its white feet. Because they live in or near waterfalls croaks wouldn't be heard. We can also signal to each other in a similar way with two flags. We call these signals semaphore (*sem-uh-for*).

- Only two types of frog live in water all their lives. Only one type of frog lives out of water all of its life (even as a tadpole). These three types of frog all live in Australia.

Microscopic Water Animals & other Pond Creepy-Crawlies

As we are animals that live mainly on land, the most obvious animals to us are those that share the land with us. Studying land animals is also easy as we don't need any special equipment to look at most of them. Pond animals, however, present us with a problem. To find them we must look on or in the water. Looking on water is not too difficult but if the pond is big you can only look along the edges. If the animals live underwater then finding them really can be quite difficult. Unless breathing apparatus is used, it is impossible to stay underwater. The only answer is to fish for the animals with a net. In this way we can hope to catch something, and by putting it in a tank or aquarium we can see what we have caught and try to find out how it lives. So, let us see what we can expect to find in a pond when we go fishing for creepy-crawlies.

Ponds in Britain are rather rare now and some are even neglected or poisoned by people dumping rubbish in them. Luckily a few people do look after their ponds and some gardeners build new ones. If the pond is clean and fresh you will find the water is full of life of all shapes and sizes. There are certainly many different sorts of plant, including the smallest, algae (al-gee), which turn the water green if there are too many of them but actually come in various colours of blue-green, yellow-green and green and red. The largest pond plants can include many reeds and even trees like the willow. There are also animals, including larger types such as birds (often ducks and geese but more unusual examples like kingfishers can sometimes be seen) and, of course, fish. But this is a book about creepy-crawlies so here is a list of the small animals you might expect to find.

1. Microscopic animals
2. Sponges
3. Hydra
4. Worms
5. Wheel animals
6. Hairy backs
7. Molluscs
8. Water bears
9. Insects and other relatives
10. Amphibians

As you can see it is quite a long list with some interesting names. The creatures are just as interesting as their names, but they can be very difficult to find and even harder to see as many are smaller than 3mm(⅛"). Insects and their relatives, amphibians and hydra, are described elsewhere in this book, but let us look at the other types of small animals.

Microscopic animals are very important to the pond. Millions of them keep the pond clean by eating many of the tiny bits of rotting, dead animal that lie on the muddy bottom. They also eat the algae that would otherwise turn the water green and eventually fill the pond, killing almost everything else. The smallest of these animals are called protozoa (*proe-toe-zoe-ah*) and consist of only one cell. All living creatures are made of cells. A house is made of bricks and by using them cleverly and using different types of brick we can build a different type of room or building. We are made of millions of cells which are used in a similar way to house bricks. Different cells make skin or muscles or blood. Simple animals have fewer cells and fewer types of cell. The simplest animals have only one cell. Most of these single-celled animals move around but a few stick to plants or rocks. Although they often eat plants or dead animals, a few will eat each other. To reproduce they often just split in half to make two new animals. If the pond dries up they can protect themselves by making a hard, dry coat which they stay inside until rain makes a new pond or they are blown into another pond. The best known of these animals are *Amoeba* (*uh-mee-bah*), *Paramecium* (*para-mee-see-um*) and *Euglena* (*you-glee-nah*). If you want to see them follow the instructions at the end of this chapter.

Sponges are things that everyone knows of but few people realize are animals. The sponge you use in the bath may be the remains of dead animals from the sea and each natural sponge would have been the home of thousands of tiny animals. Most sponges live in the sea but a few do live in freshwater, making tiny homes which would be far too small to use in a bath. They eat by letting lots of water pass through them. As it does so any tiny bits of food, including algae and microscopic animals, are filtered out and eaten. These sponges are usually grey or yellow but can be

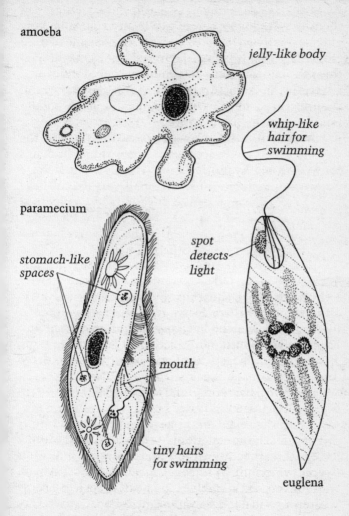

amoeba

jelly-like body

whip-like hair for swimming

paramecium

spot detects light

stomach-like spaces

mouth

tiny hairs for swimming

euglena

Some microscopic water animals

green. The green colour is not their own. Tiny algae can live inside the sponge, sharing its home (algae can also live in hydra as you will learn in the following chapter). If two living things live together and both do well by sharing, their relationship has the special name of symbiosis (sim-by-oh-sis). Algae and sponges help each other, so this is an example of symbiosis. Lots of animals live inside sponges but not all of them help the sponge.

Worms have their own chapter elsewhere in the book but it concentrates on earthworms. In ponds there are plenty of other types. The most common are flatworms which are usually small, very flat and have two eye spots on the head. If you lift up a small rock from underwater and look at the underneath side of it, you will probably find some sliding over the surface. Flatworms eat other animals.

Roundworms are long, thin, transparent and round. You can tell if you find one because they swim by frantically lashing themselves about. Not a lot is known about them. Hairworms are much longer and are grey or brown. The young live inside other animals. The adults never eat, they just create more young hairworms. The other worms you can observe are called true worms and include the earthworm. Flatworms, hairworms and some types of true worm can all be found in ponds.

Wheel animals are properly called rotifers (row-tea-firs). The largest are only 2mm long. A wheel-like part of their body near the head moves to force water past the mouth. This helps the animal feed and swim. A few attach themselves to a plant or rock and some even live inside a tube. For their size they are very complicated and well worth looking at, but because

water bear

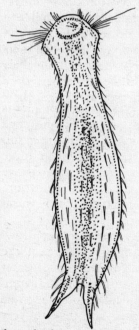

hairy back

wheel animal

they are so small you will need a microscope. Your friendly science teacher may be of help.

Hairy backs are tiny animals that feed on anything that will fit into their mouths. They move about by crawling slowly, and like most other tiny pond animals can shelter inside a tough, specially made skin if the pond dries up. Their bodies are divided into parts we call the head, neck, body and toes. Their backs may be covered in scales but are often covered in spines that make them look hairy.

Molluscs on land all have either one shell (snails) or are naked (slugs). Underwater molluscs can also have a shell made of two separate pieces joined by a hinge. Underwater snails with one shell are very similar to their land relatives and may occasionally visit the surface for air. They eat by scraping food with their many teeth. Molluscs with a hinged shell, bivalves (*bye-valves*), are different. Unlike the others they have no teeth because they filter water to get their food. This filtered water also provides them with all the oxygen they need for breathing. Cockles and mussels are the most common types of freshwater bivalves. Pet shops occasionally sell them. They are very similar to the cockles and mussels sold by fishmongers (which come from the sea).

Water bears are tubby little creatures that move like a bear and so are given their name. They have eight hooked legs. They will live through any sort of weather, however bad, even if their surroundings completely dry out. They do this by making a temporary shell or cyst (*sist*) inside of which they stay. The cyst stops them drying out completely. They do not move or eat until they find themselves in a pond again.

Identifying Microscopic Water Animals

You will need
- pond water
- a dropper
- some plasticine
- glass or plastic microscope slides
- a microscope
- a glass or plastic container

What to do

Collect a small amount of pond water in your container. Sit at a table with your microscope and make sure that when you look down it you can see light. If your microscope has a built-in light this will make things very easy. If not, you will need to move the small mirror at the bottom until it reflects light from a window or a light bulb into the microscope.

Take a small piece of plasticine and roll it into a very thin sausage. Make a small ring with the sausage and put the ring on the slide in the middle. Press slightly to make sure it sticks. Now use your dropper to put a very small amount of pond water, preferably just one drop, on the slide inside the ring. The plasticine ring will stop the water running away. Now put another slide on top and press it. The water and plasticine will be sandwiched between the two slides and the water will not be able to escape.

Now put the slide sandwich on the microscope and use the focus controls to move the eyepiece up or down until you can see the creatures in the water. By comparing what you see with the illustrations on pages 89 and 91, you should be able to see what animals you have in the pond water. You will also find it fun to see how they move.

Cheap microscopes and slides are usually sold in

good toy shops, hobby shops and large department stores (if they sell toys). If you cannot find a good, cheap microscope in any shop, the names and addresses of some manufacturers are given at the back of the book. Try writing to them and ask if they can tell you where you can buy their microscope. Do try locally first.

Did You Know

- Hairworms were thought to be created from horses' hairs. People thought that when a hair dropped off a horse's tail and fell into water, it turned into a live worm!

- Almost all wheel animals are females. Males are born only if there are too many females in the pond, if there is too little water or if the weather gets very cold. Males are used only for reproduction so they never eat, not even when they are born.

- Hairy backs in freshwater are always female. There are never any males. They breed by parthenogenesis, a method also used by greenfly and bees.

- Water fleas have only one eye.

12 Hydra

Have you ever heard of a mythological lady called the Gorgon? In fact there wasn't just one, there were three, and they were a terrible trio of sisters to look upon. Almost everything about them was fairly normal except for their hair. They didn't have any. Instead their heads were covered in live snakes that wriggled and writhed making the sisters look really hideous. Even hideous doesn't really describe how terrifying they looked. The sisters terrified almost everyone because they looked very frightening but, worse still, if you were silly enough to look at any one of them the shock was meant to turn you into stone! The terrible sisters were supposed to have existed thousands of years ago in the days when the centre of civilization was Greece, and of the three, the most famous was called Medusa.

Now I suppose you are wondering what three hideous sisters have to do with creepy-crawlies. Well there are some animals that remind people of the sisters. They are called coelenterates (*see-lent-or-ates*) and consist of two main parts. The body is really just a large stomach. All that is attached to the body is a head which consists of a mouth and thousands of deadly tentacles that look just like snakes. It is these snake-like tentacles that caused scientists to remember the story of the Gorgons and, in particular, Medusa. In jellyfish and corals the babies are even called medusae (*med-you-zee*) after that hideous sister. Adult sea anemones and hydra are even more like the Medusa of Greek mythology. They are still like jellyfish except that they have a stalk or foot that can hold on to anything solid.

Coelenterates always live in water, but while most of their relatives live in the sea, hydra are always found in freshwater. They live in ponds that have lots of healthy plants and other water life. They like to fix themselves to something solid like a stone or a plant and their foot, which is like a sucker, helps them do this. Once fixed to their home they become a deadly enemy to anything smaller that dares to swim by. For although hydra will seldom grow much larger than

3cm(1") in length, the tentacles on their head hold hundreds of stinging cells each of which can kill, even if only slightly touched. Each sting has a tiny trigger like a hair. If any animal should move the hair the sting explodes, sending something very much like a whip flying out towards the prey. The end of the whip is very sharp and usually goes straight into the animal. Small hooks on the end make it almost impossible for the animal to get away – only large fish manage to escape. Once caught, the struggling victim is dragged by the tentacles towards the mouth and finally pushed into the stomach while still alive. There is no escape now. The invitation to dinner is permanent with no choice of what to eat. Some of these creepy-crawlies really are quite nasty, aren't they?

You may already think hydra are a bit odd, but wait until you hear how they have babies. At first a female hydra will look a bit like a tube with tentacles at one end. Then a bump grows somewhere on the side. Next little bumps grow on the end of the bump, and these slowly turn into tentacles. Suddenly the end of the bump with the tentacles grows a hole in its middle. Finally this bump, with its tentacles and hole, drops off the parent hydra! There you have it, a baby hydra which looks just like mum, but smaller. In case you are interested, the proper name for the bump is a bud and this way of growing babies is called budding.

Hydra can also produce babies in another way. This other, less common, way also begins as a bump on a parent hydra. The bump swells like a pimple until it bursts, releasing millions of tiny sperm into the water. These sperm must swim to find another hydra, but the second hydra will also have a bump. One of the sperm must enter this bump (it isn't the same type as the one that burst) to fertilize it. If this happens the bump grows until it bursts, but this time a ball comes out and falls to the bottom of the pond. Later this ball grows into a baby hydra which starts life with just two tentacles. Unfortunately for the other pond animals, these two tentacles are still deadly.

How hydra reproduce

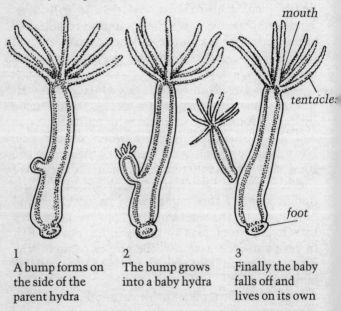

mouth

tentacles

foot

1
A bump forms on the side of the parent hydra

2
The bump grows into a baby hydra

3
Finally the baby falls off and lives on its own

Hydra can move in one of three ways. To demonstrate one way, begin by standing up straight. Bend over and put your hands on the ground as far away as you can without falling over. Shuffle your feet until they touch your hands (but don't take your feet off the ground). Now stand up straight. You have just 'looped', which is a hydra's favourite way of moving. Hydra also move by somersaulting head over heels, although they don't do this often. Finally, hydra can catch hold of an air bubble and simply float away. They use the air bubble in just the same way that we use a hot air balloon, but this method is only used very rarely.

How To Keep Hydra

You will need

a fish tank or large jar	fine gravel
a nearby pond	aquarium plants
another jar	water fleas or similar
a fishing net	animals

What to do

Many ponds in Britain are now protected by law (which is a very good thing), so be sure to find out whether the one you choose is protected. If the pond is protected you must not remove anything from it. In this case try asking local farmers or the local council if they know of a pond you can use. If they don't, your school biology teacher will probably be able to help get some hydra. When you find a pond, get permission from the owner and then collect a small amount of the weed that grows underwater. You may need to use a fishing net or stick to reach the weed. Put the weed in a jar and fill it with water from the pond. Put the jar down and look at the weed for a small bump that looks like jelly. To find any hydra on the weed you will need to wait until the water stops moving. If a hydra is there it will carefully begin to stretch out both its body and its arms after several minutes. If you haven't found any after about five minutes, put all the weed back in the pond and start again with fresh weed. You may need to look in more than one pond to find any hydra.

When you have found some hydra, keep them and the weed they are on in the jar of water until you get home. Then prepare your large jar or fish tank. Put a layer of fine gravel on the bottom of the jar or tank (you can buy this at most good pet shops). Fill up the tank with water. It is best to use water from the same pond as the hydra, but rain-water will also do. If you have to use tap water, boil it first, and leave it until it is cold again. It should then be fit to use.

When the tank is full of water, put a few plants in it. Again you can get these in pet shops that sell tropical fish, but they are also available from plant shops that sell pond plants. The easiest plant to grow is Canadian pond weed (*Elodea*). Also add a stone or small rock to the tank. Finally add the piece of weed with the hydra on it. Now put the tank or large jar in a nice bright place but not where the sun will shine on it. Your hydra home is now finished and all you must ensure is that there is always a full tank of water and that you remember to feed the hydra. Any small animals that swim in the water will do. Water fleas (*Daphnia*) are excellent. Catch them in a pond with a fine net or buy them in a pet or tropical fish shop. Whichever food you use, it must be alive. Let it swim around. The hydra will catch it.

Did You Know

- The three Gorgon sisters were called Stheno, Euryale and Medusa.

- Perseus killed one of the sisters, Medusa, by cutting off her head with a sword. He didn't dare look at her for fear of turning to stone, so he used his shiny shield as a mirror and looked only at her reflection.

- Hydra and its relatives are made almost entirely of water.

- Hydra usually look red, green or brown, but in fact they are transparent and have no colour of their own. Tiny algae, coloured red, green or brown, live inside the hydra in what for them is an ideal home. The algae grow using carbon dioxide from the hydra which is pleased to get rid of it.

13 Bees

You and I are used to talking to other people. It's something we do most of the time and often without really thinking. It allows us to ask people how they are, whether something tastes nice, how to get somewhere, or for help. Talking is a way of communicating, but there are other ways. Other noises can be used. For example, a scream usually means someone has been shocked or frightened. A silent smile can mean that someone wants to be friendly.

People are generally very good at communicating, but so are other animals. Monkeys have quite a complicated language relying mainly on movements of the face and body but also on a few sounds. Dolphins and whales have a very complicated sound language, and so do birds with their songs. As there are plenty of different types of animal that can communicate, perhaps it isn't such a surprise to find some very small creatures that manage just as well – they are the bees.

Bees are notable, along with their relatives the wasps and ants, for forming colonies. These are large collections of animals all of which work together for the common good. Although bees are mainly colonial animals, there are some that prefer to live most of their life alone. An example is the Potter Flower Bee which is a rather primitive type of bee. Bees probably all preferred to live by themselves millions of years ago, when they first appeared on our planet. Some of them learnt to help each other in small ways and obviously this made their lives easier. So if something bad happened, say the food was poor one year, the bees that survived would probably be the ones with the easier lives, the ones that helped each other. This is probably what happened to create the Potter Flower Bee. It still lives by itself except when breeding. Then it mates and finds a suitable place for a nest near lots more of its kind. There it builds a simple nest of its own from clay. The nest is close to, but not touching, nests of other bees. After the eggs have been laid in the nests, all the bees leave and return to living alone. While the bees are all together they do perform one colonial or common act. They all protect all the nests from any attackers. This is therefore an example of a very simple and early type of temporary colony.

Bumble-bees demonstrate the next development in the colonial life of bees. They form permanent colonies where all the bees stay together until the end of the year. Then all of them, except the new queens, die. Each queen hibernates through winter and starts a new colony in spring. She builds oval cells made of beeswax which she kneads with pollen and resin. The cells are filled with pollen or honey and each then has several eggs added. The eggs hatch into maggots which eat the food in their cell. Then the queen feeds them from other honey-filled cells. These maggots all turn into very special female bees. They are not queens and cannot mate or lay eggs. Instead they are infertile females used as workers for the colony. They now begin to take over from the queen, collecting food and feeding the young. This leaves the queen free to lay more and more eggs. In summer, instead of worker bees, the maggots hatch into males and fertile females. The males mate with the fertile females and die. The fertile females become the queens for the next year and prepare to hibernate while the other bees die. The whole cycle then repeats itself.

Wasps and hornets are very similar to bumble-bees in their lifestyle. They have bigger colonies and tend to steal their food, often from other bees, including the bumble-bee. Their egg and storage cells are usually made of paper which they make by chewing wood. Wasps, hornets and bumble-bees have well-developed colonies as different types of animals have different jobs to do. Queens reproduce and build the first nest (or hive), infertile females act as workers, and males just help in producing new queens.

Honey bees have the most advanced colonies of all the bees. Here the whole colony lasts for several years and the bees have very special jobs to do, depending on what type of bee they are and how old they are. A colony contains about 40,000 to 70,000 workers (infertile females), some drones (males) and a single queen. The workers are created by the queen in a process that doesn't need males or fertilization. It is called parthenogenesis (described in the chapter on greenfly). When a worker bee changes from a maggot into an adult, its first job is to clean the hive and keep it fresh. On the fourth day it turns to feeding maggots with a special liquid it makes called pap. As the maggot grows the worker adds different amounts of

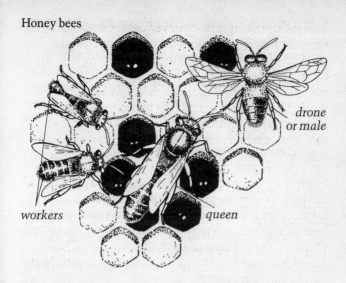

drone
or male

workers

queen

honey and pollen to the pap. From the tenth day to
the twentieth, the worker helps build and repair the
hive using glands in its body to make waxy cells
called beeswax. It uses its jaws to knead the wax and
moulds it into perfectly hexagonal (six-sided) cells.
No one knows how the workers manage to build the
cells so well that they are all the same size, shape and
thickness. Twenty-day-old workers move on to
guarding the entrance. They also point their bottoms
into the air and give off a scent that attracts the other
members of the hive back, and part of their time is
spent going out to collect pollen and nectar. Amazingly, if too many bees die, any other bee can do its
job. If necessary a replacement bee will be found. If it
is too young it will mature very quickly. If it is too old
it will appear to get younger! Workers have a busy but
short life, usually dying after a few weeks.

The drones are only used for mating. Whether or not they succeed in mating with a queen, they are all driven out of the hive or killed after the mating flight has finished. The hive is carefully controlled so that it is always at (or within half a degree of) the right temperature of 35°C. Workers use their wings as fans and also fill central cells with water to help cool the hive. If heating is needed they shiver to increase the temperature. In winter the hive is allowed to fall to 20°C while the bees huddle together for warmth. From time to time the coldest bees on the outside of the huddle change places with warmer bees on the inside. When there are several queens and too many bees in a hive, the oldest queen will fly off with some of the workers to start a new hive.

As you can see, the hive is quite complicated with lots of different jobs for everyone. It really is a very advanced colony but there is still more to know about these astonishing creatures. The bees have their own language which they use to tell each other where there is food. It is called a dance and is performed by the workers who go out for food. When they return to the hive they find a place to dance and other bees watch. As they dance they wiggle. If they are walking straight up (imagine they are on your wall) while wiggling, it means the bees must fly straight towards the sun to find food. If they walk up at an angle, it means fly at this angle to the sun. At the same time, for each set of wiggles the bee also walks in a circle (to start the wiggles again). The slower the circles, the longer the bees must fly to reach the food. So, the wiggles tell other bees what direction to fly in and the circles tell them how far to fly. Amazing, isn't it?

Building A Home For Bees

You will need

    a clean tin can (open at one end only)

    a pair of scissors

    a packet of large drinking straws (that is, with wide holes)

    silicone rubber glue

What to do

Be careful not to use a can with a sharp edge, and make sure it is clean and dry. Take one of the drinking straws and put it in the can. Use the scissors to carefully cut the straw so that it is just long enough to fit in the can. Remember, scissors can be dangerous so take care when using them. Take the piece of straw out of the can and cut all the other straws to the same length as the first one.

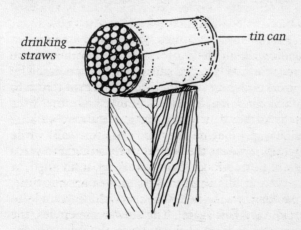

drinking straws — tin can

Now put all the straws into the can until there is no room for any more. Do not force them in but make sure they cannot move about, or easily fall out. Now glue the can on to a tree between two branches, or on to a fence-post. If necessary you may have to buy a fence-post and ask an adult to fix it firmly for you, but even small bushes can hold your bee home quite well.

If you do this in early spring you should eventually see one or two bees make their home inside the straws. Only solitary bees that like to live alone will choose to live in it. They will probably be Leaf-Cutter or Mason bees. As long as you watch them without annoying them they will almost certainly ignore you. You can therefore enjoy watching them build their home and coming and going in search of food.

Did You Know

- Hornets have the most painful sting of any European bee.

- Killer bees do exist. The fiercest bees are found in Africa. Unlike most bees, they are very strong and can sting many times. The sting is very painful but small numbers of African bees can do enough damage to actually kill. American killer bees were created accidentally by man. African bees were taken to South America by scientists who were hoping to use them to breed strong bees that were peaceful. The idea was to mate the African strong (and fierce) bee with South American peaceful (and weak) bees. Unfortunately, before the scientists had succeeded, a few bees accidentally escaped and bred with wild bees, producing very strong, very fierce bees. Now North America is slowly being invaded by these bees and although there haven't as yet been any scenes like those portrayed in some films, they are certainly dangerous enough for people to worry about.

- Bees can't fly! Well, that's what engineers say. According to people who study how to make aeroplanes fly, a bee and its wings are the wrong size and shape and should never be able to fly. So, the next time you see a bee buzz past you, remind it that it can't fly! Obviously, as bees *do* fly the engineers must be wrong.

- Some wasps hunt spiders. They are immune to the spider's bite and poison and sting the spider to paralyse it. The spiders are dragged back to the nest and eggs are laid on or near the still live, paralysed spiders. When the maggots hatch, all the spider can do is watch the maggots crawl towards it for lunch.

- Bees can see the sun even on a cloudy day. Their eyes are adapted to see light differently from ours. They must find flowers in cloudy or bright weather. To do this they use mostly blue light, including ultraviolet which we cannot see.

14 Ants

Of all the animals in the world, human beings have created the most complex communities. To keep so many people happy, even when living very close to each other, we have invented all sorts of rules. Some of these are never written down. To see an example of one of these at work, find a friend and walk up to him or her until your face is about 3cm(1″) away from theirs (but do not touch). They probably will not let you get that near, or if they do they will look very uncomfortable. There is an unwritten rule that allows us to keep our privacy. Subconsciously, our minds pretend that the area around us is private and everyone else must stay out. Generally, if you enter someone's area they will back off, look very unhappy or perhaps even threaten you. At the same time, because you don't want someone in your area, normally you will not go too close to others. In this way we spend a lot of our time avoiding fights, which is obviously a good thing. Of course there are some written rules. We call them laws. They are also devised to prevent fights and unhappiness.

Another reason why human communities are generally well organized and can build enormous cities is that everyone has their own special role to play. Think of all the people you know who work. There are shopkeepers, miners, typists, cooks, cleaners, farmers and thousands of other jobs, and each person does only one (or sometimes a few). No one does everything.

This sharing of the work so that each individual is a specialist is what makes a community or colony. A large group of animals couldn't survive together without all helping in some way. We know we are colonial animals of an incredibly advanced kind. Bees, described elsewhere in this book, are also colonial animals. In this chapter, we are going to look at yet another example. They are probably the most advanced colonial creatures of all, excluding ourselves. They are the ants.

Ants are members of a group of insects called the hymenoptera (*high-men-op-turr-ah*) which also includes wasps and bees. They are almost all colonial animals. All ants are colonial and share out the work in a nest to a high degree. The individuals are excellently designed to do their particular jobs.

A single nest will often contain several queens, the females who lay eggs. They are served by female workers and small males, but the nest actually starts with a queen which has mated. A queen is fertilized during a special time in spring when all the kings (or males) and queens fly together in what is called a nuptial flight. When she has been fertilized, the queen lands and breaks off her own wings. The muscles used for flying will never be used again so they often dissolve in the body to be used as food. She may also lay and eat some eggs. In this way the queen can live without hunting for food. She will usually hunt for a stone or something else to live under. Just think of all the places other creepy-crawlies would like and that's where you will find ants. When the queen has found somewhere to hide, she will lay and look after her first eggs. These will hatch into females and will be the new workers. They cannot and will never be able to mate.

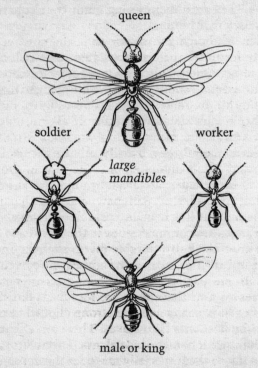

queen

soldier

large mandibles

worker

male or king

The infertile females are usually divided into several different types and actually look different. Although there may be more, two types are predominant. The smaller ones are normal workers. Some will fetch food while others will keep the nest clean or look after the young. Larger females usually have incredibly large jaws or mandibles (*man-dibbles*) that are used to defend the nest from attack. Such large females are called soldiers and do not just defend the nest, but also help hunt. Males are usually the smallest ants but unlike male bees, they are allowed to live. They are born in spring, ready to take part in the mating flight.

When it is time for mating to begin, the queen, already fertilized that previous year, lays two new types of egg. One will create winged females, soon to become queens, and the other will produce winged males or kings. The young queens and kings fly off together in a muddled swarm quite unlike the orderly bee swarm (which also contains workers). After the ants have mated they usually fall to the ground exhausted. The males often die. The rest, including some of the females, are eaten by animals. The few females that survive will now become the new queens and start the new life cycle all over again.

Ant nests are common all over the world and are found in almost any suitable place, such as under stones, in leaf piles, in trees and houses. In some cases the ants are parasitic – they take over other ant colonies so that their nests are found inside other ants' nests! Amazon ants are strong enough also to make the host ants their slaves. There are also ants that make their homes inside plants. The plants have spaces inside them specially made for the ants and a small hole grows to make a door. The ants move in to their home and then protect the plant from being eaten by biting hungry animals. Many a human plant-hunter has been surprised to pick up a plant and suddenly find their hand is being savagely bitten by hundreds of tiny ants. Orchids and air plants (relatives of the pineapple) are just two of the plants ants sometimes choose to live in.

Each ant or ant species is very well designed for its way of life. Ants are basically runners as their legs are long and thin and have no suckers. Surprisingly, running is not common in insects. Even though some ants have wings they are very poor flyers, often crashing into each other and falling to their deaths. They can protect themselves and each other in a variety of ways including biting, stinging and squirting acid. Most ants are blind.

Making A Formicarium

You will need

a metal tin lid (e.g. 32cm × 32cm[12″ × 12″] biscuit-tin lid)
plaster of Paris
sand
a small bottle
water
an ants' nest
a small saw
a spoon
soil and sand
cotton wool

a 5mm × 10mm(¼″ × ½″) piece of wood, nearly as long as the tin
plastic insulating tape
transparent perspex (same size as tin lid)
a brush (such as a paintbrush)
food
black paper
a pencil
water
piece of white paper or card

What to do

Mix the plaster of Paris (powder) with water. Make a

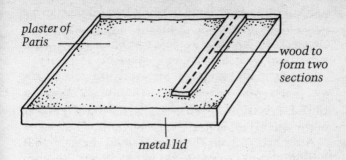

plaster of Paris

wood to form two sections

metal lid

Top view

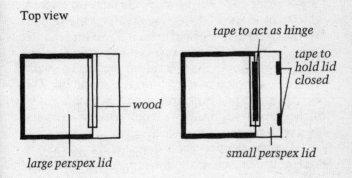

tape to act as hinge

tape to hold lid closed

wood

large perspex lid

small perspex lid

Side view

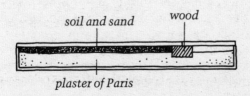

soil and sand

wood

plaster of Paris

paste stiff enough so that it sticks to a spoon and doesn't fall off when you turn it upside down. Pour the plaster paste into your tin lid. A large biscuit-tin lid measuring about 32cm × 32cm(12″ × 12″) will be a good size. Pour in enough plaster so that when it is levelled it comes to within 2 or 3mm(⅛″) of the top of the lid. Try to build the edges up to the top of the sides of the tin lid (but definitely not higher).

After half an hour the plaster should be damp but beginning to go solid. If it is not too runny you can position the piece of wood. This should be just shorter than the side of the lid. If your lid is 32cm long, a 30cm piece will be ideal. On one of the 10mm wide sides mark a dotted line all along the middle. Put the wood in the lid and press it down into the wet plaster so that the dotted line is uppermost. One end of the wood should touch a side of the lid. The wood should be about 4cm from one edge of the lid. This will divide the lid into a large and a small section. Use the perspex to press the wood down so that its top is level with the top of the lid.

Make sure the perspex is covering the lid exactly. Stick a strip of tape on the perspex so that one edge of the tape marks the position of the dotted line you drew on the wood. Remove the perspex and use the saw to cut along the tape edge to make two separate pieces (ask an adult to help you with this – SAWS ARE DANGEROUS). Make sure the plaster is still damp and add a few splashes of water if necessary. Now fill the large section with a mixture of soil and sand. Put the large piece of perspex over the large section. Tape the three edges touching the tin with the insulating tape to hold the perspex in place. Then put the small piece of perspex over the small section of the lid. Use more tape to join the two pieces of perspex together where they touch. This should make a hinge so the small piece of perspex can be opened or closed as a door. You can use small pieces of tape to help hold this door closed. You have now made an ant home which is called a formicarium (*form-ee-care-ee-um*).

Go outside with the formicarium, white paper or card, bottle and brush and find an ants' nest. Make sure the ants are not a fierce variety (avoid red ants). It will need to be a small nest that is very shallow. Try looking under stones. When you find one, quickly use the brush to collect the ants and eggs carefully on to the paper and into the small chamber of the formicarium. As soon as some are inside shut the door or they will escape. Now collect the rest in the bottle. When you need to, quickly empty the ants from the bottle into the formicarium and start collecting again. Collect all the ants and eggs but do not mix ants from different nests. When all the ants are trapped you can cover both pieces of perspex with black paper using more tape. Leave the ants on a flat surface where it is not too hot. They will build a new nest in the soil. After one day you can supply the ants with food and water. Damp cotton wool will provide the water. For food you can add insects, worms, honey or jam. Put these in the small section.

By lifting up the black paper you can watch your ants as they build, search for food, communicate with each other and look after their young. If the small space gets too dirty you can clean it out. Also make sure the soil is slightly damp by taking off the perspex (outdoors) and wetting it just a little. You will need to do this only about once a month. Be careful not to let the ants escape when you do this. The darker it is, the less the ants are likely to try. In late summer, let the ants go outside. You can start again next year.

If you are very short of space you can use the wormery as an ant home, but do take the worms out first, and remember to fit a lid.

Plaster of Paris can be bought in home-decorating shops. Insulation tape is available in electrical departments and DIY shops and perspex is available in DIY shops or glass merchants.

Did You Know

- South American Leaf-Cutter ants are farmers. They search for leaves and cut them into small pieces. These are carried back to the nest and into the underground farm. A fungus is injected into the leaves and allowed to .grow. The fungus is continually fed by the ants. The ants then eat the fungus. Without the fungus the ants would starve to death. The fungus is found only in ants' nests.

- A nest or colony of wood ants can contain up to 100,000 ants.

- In some countries wood ants are protected by law so it is illegal to hurt or kill them. They help kill caterpillars that would otherwise damage crops, including trees.

- Honey Pot ants live on honey. Some of the colony's ants store the honey in their bodies and so swell up. They become so large that they look like balloons with legs. Sometimes they hold so much honey their body explodes!

- Ants 'talk' by rubbing their antennae together.

- Weaver ants make their nests inside leaves that they sew together with silk.

- Bulldog ants have stings that are 1cm(½") long, and they can also jump several centimetres.   .

- Pharoe ants are less than ½mm long.

- If every single animal in the world was the same size, ants would be the strongest.

15 Spiders

In this book there are several different examples of insects, including the ladybird, cockroach and bee, and we know that they share a common characteristic in having six legs. Another look at them will tell us a bit more about insects. If you look at a dead fly you will easily see that the body is very hard. Compare that with our own bodies and you realize we are generally quite soft but have hard bones inside us. So the bodies of insects are the reverse of our own by having the soft parts inside and the 'bones' outside. They are not really bones but they do the same job of supporting and protecting the body and so form a skeleton. Once an animal has a hard skeleton it can have joints to help it move. Your joints are parts such as your elbow, knee, knuckle and neck. Insects have similar joints, though not as many. Insect bodies are also divided into three obvious sections. So we see that all insects share not one but several characteristics, including a hard outer skeleton, three body segments, and joints. Now it is time to learn about another animal that shares these characteristics and is therefore closely related to insects.

If there has ever been a creepy-crawly that could

frighten more people than any other, surely it must be the spider. These common creatures are found all over the world and although very few are able to harm us, they are often hated or feared. The reasons for hating them are quite strange. Most people will say they hate spiders because they are big and hairy, but you are also big and hairy, so why don't people hate you? Another common excuse is that spiders are poisonous. Although spiders do have a really nasty bite, which is dangerous if you are an insect, most of them cannot even hurt us. It is true that some are poisonous or have really bad bites. For example, the Bird-Eating spider is pretty big and hairy and the bite will definitely hurt, but it isn't likely to kill you. It is not very often you would come across one of these spiders, but if you did, it is more than likely it would run away rather than attack what it thinks is a gigantic, ugly monster – YOU! In fact, you are far more likely to be or become very ill from contact with some of the flies that live near us, than by most spiders.

As you have already read, spiders are relatives of insects and share three characteristics with them. Firstly, they have a hard skeleton on the outside of their body. It is as if you had all your bones taken out and then covered yourself in a suit of armour that was stuck to you. The skeleton, whether outside or inside, is used to support the body which would otherwise resemble a wobbly jelly. The proper name for a skeleton outside the body is an exoskeleton (*ex-oh-skell-ee-tonn*). Secondly, the legs have joints so they can bend only at particular places, just like yours and mine. Thirdly, the body is divided into three parts. However, despite being similar to insects, spiders are different in some important ways. Although their bodies do have three sections, the third one (the abdomen) is hidden under the rest of the body and the first two sections (the head and thorax) are joined together so that they look like one. A more obvious difference is that whereas insects have six legs, spiders have eight. All animals with a hard outer body and joints are called arthropods (*are-throw-pods*). Those with six legs are insects, those with ten are crustaceans (such as wood lice), but if they have eight they are spiders (a few other very similar creatures, which include the mites, also have eight legs).

All spiders are carnivores and eat meat that they have caught. They have a remarkable number of ways of catching their prey. Trapdoor spiders hide in a hole with a lid on it until something tasty comes too near.

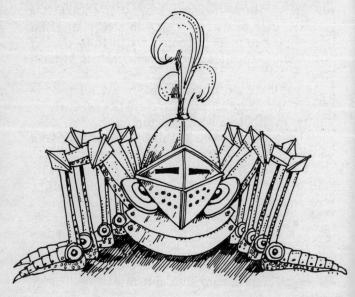

The spider then opens the trap door, catches the animal and goes back into its hole – all in less than one second. Orb-spinning spiders use a web as a sort of sticky fishing-net to catch flies or, in the case of the Bird-Eating spider, birds! Jumping spiders have fantastic eyesight and wait for their prey to come into sight before jumping next to or on to it to catch it.

One spider makes a sticky bolas. A bolas is a South American hunting weapon made from three pieces of string and three stones. If thrown properly it spins horizontally like a wheel and either the stones knock the animal out when they hit it or, more usually, the string wraps itself around the animal and stops it from moving until the hunter can catch up with it. The spider makes one long thread with a sticky blob on the end of it. While suspending itself in the air on another thread, it swings the bolas round underneath it. Moths are attracted by the noise of the bolas turning in the air and get stuck to it if they go too near. All the spider has to do then is reel in the thread like a fisherman and either eat its victim or package it away to eat later. Yet another spider spits at its prey. Each spit causes sticky glue to shoot out, and if any touches the prey (usually insects) it pins and sticks the creature to the ground. The prey then has to wait for the spider to run up and eat it. There are many other ways spiders trap their food, but whichever method is used the end is always similar. If the spider is very hungry it bites the still-living creature and sucks all the blood out of it. If it isn't that hungry the spider bites the animal and injects it with a chemical that paralyses, but doesn't kill it. The animal is then put somewhere safe to be eaten alive some time later.

If you want to keep spiders you are going to find it

difficult unless you keep just one. A hungry spider is not a very friendly creature. In fact, it is not really very friendly even when it is full. Most of the time it will quite happily attack other spiders, and if it is hungry it can be cannibalistic and eat them. If you still want to try, put some sticks or twigs in a glass or plastic jar (or fish tank), or better still, make a small garden inside a fish tank with earth and living plants. Just put in a layer of earth and plant any small plants you like. If you buy these from a garden centre and ask for plants suitable for a bottle garden, they will always remain small enough for your tank or jar. Catch just one spider and put it in the container. Now put on a tight-fitting lid (plastic or metal) that has some small air holes in it. If necessary, make your own small air holes using a nail, but do ask an adult to help you. If the spider is very small, or you hope to get baby spiders, you should use a lid made of cotton sheet, held in place with elastic. You can use the 'cage' you made for caterpillars, if you like. Feed the spider every week, perhaps twice a week, with a large fly or maggot put in its web. Catch the fly outside with a net or ask a friend who goes fishing for a maggot. If you like, you can put a few maggots in the tank and let them hatch. Then the flies might fly into the web by themselves. Garden spiders are generally harmless, but if you think spiders near where you live can be poisonous, ask an adult for advice. Do let your spider go after a few weeks or at the end of the summer.

An Experiment With A Spider's Web

You will need

a small spray gun	a roll of black and
a camera	white film
a spider with its web	some black paper
some tracing paper	a pencil
several garden sticks	a tiny piece of white
water	paper

What to do

On a nice warm day find a spider and its web in the garden. Use the spray gun full of water to spray the web gently without damaging it. You can use a small spray that is designed for spraying indoor plants or perfume. Covered with tiny water droplets, the web will look beautiful, but the reason for doing this is to make it easier to see. Take a photograph of the web. If you have to borrow a camera, get an adult to show you how to use it and to help you take the photos to avoid wasting film. You do not need to be able to see anything else in the photograph, so get as close as your camera will allow to include most or all of the web. Try asking a friend to hold some black paper behind the web (without touching it) to make sure that it appears clearly in the photograph. It might be a good idea to take several different photos from slightly different places. Place sticks in the ground to mark where your toes were when you took the photos. The wet web is quite useless to the spider so it will eat it and remake it, but just to make sure use a twig or something else convenient to gently make a big hole in the middle of the web. Leave the spider alone for the rest of the day, but put another bigger stick in the ground near the web so you can find it again.

Next day return to where the spider's web was (look for the second stick). It should have built another one. If it hasn't, try leaving it for another day and check again. If it still hasn't rebuilt the web, you will have to start the experiment again with a new spider. When you do find a replacement web, put a tiny piece of paper on to it, near (but not directly in) the middle, and use your spray to wet the web again. Take some more photographs just like the previous ones, making sure your toes are in the same positions you marked with the sticks.

Get your photographs developed. When you get them back, divide them into two groups. The first group should be the photos of the original web, which can be identified because it doesn't have a piece of paper on it. The second group will be of the replacement web with its piece of paper. Now trace the web from any good picture in the first group. When you have finished, see if any of the webs in the second group of photos matches the tracing you have made.

You should find that the web in one of the pictures in the second group is identical or almost identical to your tracing of the original web. This happens because each spider always builds its own web in the same way. It may change size and shape very slightly but the pattern is always the same. Spiders are born with this pattern in their memories so they do not need to learn how to build a web. They only know the one way to build their web, so each time they make one it is almost identical to the last one. You are born with memories as well. From the first minute of your life you knew how to cry and smile. Memories or skills that animals are born with are said to be innate.

Watching Baby Spiders Run

You will need
a spiders' nest full of baby spiders

What to do
During summer look on plants outdoors for a nest of baby spiders. It looks like a ball made of web with lots of dark spots, the babies, inside it. The nest is quite big, usually about 1 to 3cm or more in diameter and may be large enough to cover the space between several leaves or twigs. All the babies will be tightly grouped together in one place for most of the time. All you need to do for this experiment is blow on the nest or lightly knock the bit of plant the nest is on. Watch what happens.

All the baby spiders run off very quickly in different directions. The question you should ask is why? The answer is that they do this to protect themselves from being attacked. They feel the sudden breath of air or vibration of the plant and assume it is an animal that may want to eat them. By suddenly running away, each baby might escape becoming somebody else's lunch. By all going in different directions they also do two other things. Firstly, any bigger animal will find it difficult to follow one of them as it's hard to keep your eyes on just one when fifty other spiders are also running past you. Secondly, even if the animal does successfully catch a few spiders, it can't chase all of them if they go in different directions, so some of them are bound to survive. Only when it is safe will they return to the nest.

Did You Know

- Some spiders can hang glide or fly. Small spiders climb to the top of a plant and produce a thread which they hang in the air. When the wind catches the thread, they hang on to it and let go of the plant. How far they travel depends on how high they were at the start and how strong the wind is. They can easily travel one or two metres in a gentle breeze.

- If a young spider loses a leg it can grow another.

- Spider thread is a liquid that turns sticky and solid when it leaves the spider and touches the air. The silk can be spun to make clothes.

- Other animals (such as caterpillars) can make silk but spiders use it in more ways than any other animal. They use it for lifelines, pupa cases (called cocoons), houses (including underwater houses), traps and parachutes.

- Jungle soldiers and people who live permanently in jungles have used spiders' webs as bandages. They quickly stop bleeding and help to protect an open wound.

 **Tarantulas**

Elsewhere in the book you will have read about spiders, but if you tried either of the two experiments you will probably have used common or garden spiders. Unless you live in South America or a few other places nearby, the tarantula will not be either common or in your garden, but almost everyone has heard of it. Is it the terrible creature it is meant to be? To find out read on.

The name tarantula originates from a little town in southern Italy called Taranto. Poisonous spiders sometimes used to bite people from the town and if this happened the people had a very weird cure. They used to make the injured person dance! The dance was a very wild and exciting one which used up a lot of energy. The patient was forced to dance until exhausted because it was hoped that all the poison would be sweated out. The name of this dance was the tarantella.

All this originated long before America had been discovered, so obviously, as tarantulas come from America, the poisonous spiders were not tarantulas. (In fact they were Wolf Spiders which, though quite small, are very nasty.) After America, and in particular

South America, had been discovered, explorers soon brought back tales of hot and steamy jungles full of strange and sometimes terrible creatures. One of these creatures was the now well-known Bird-Eating Spider and it became the second animal to be called a tarantula. The name was also used to refer to other species, including some spiders from North America and even some scorpions, before the large, hairy creatures we know and fear were allowed to be the owners of the name.

The tarantula is one of the best examples of a misunderstood animal. It is one of the biggest spiders, being three or four inches long, and very hairy with fangs that can easily pierce our skin to inject a painful poison. However, the poison is not strong enough to kill most healthy people and hurts about as much as a bee sting. What is more, the female tarantula is likely to bite a human being only if forced to do so. Any sensible female tarantula runs away or just stays quite still until people pass, as we are far too big to be of interest to her. Even if you do annoy one it will try to frighten you away. When very angry they may pull out the hairs on their back and throw them, hoping this will scare the attacker off. Only if this fails will they bite (unless you nearly kill or hurt one by sitting or stepping on it). On the other hand the male tarantula is truly a bad-tempered fellow. He is mostly interested in finding a female and often bites anything that gets in his way. Fortunately he is still likely to try to avoid creatures as big as humans.

Just like most other spiders, tarantulas eat insects. They are hunters rather than trappers and most of them hunt on the ground, but some, including the South American Red-Toe Tarantula, live in trees.

Although this one will hunt on the move, it prefers to hide and wait for lunch to walk by, when it pounces on its prey. In order to help it hide, and also to build a home, the tree tarantulas spin messy webs. The other tarantulas do not make webs, but dig shallow burrows in the ground to live in. All female tarantulas make silk which they use to form a cocoon or protective case around their eggs. The cocoon is carried around until the babies hatch out.

How To Keep Tarantulas

You will need

- a glass or plastic tank (with lid)
- small indoor plants or dead branches
- insects (for food)
- some cotton wool
- a female tarantula
- potting compost
- a small water dish
- a lump of cork bark
- water

What to do

The tank must be strong so the spider can't escape, and the lid must be equally strong for the same reason. An escaped tarantula isn't dangerous but it will probably scare anyone who doesn't expect to bump into it. You can use a fish tank or buy a special tank from suppliers listed at the back of the book. Put your potting compost into the tank. A good depth, say 8–10cm(3–4"), will allow the spider to burrow. The lump of bark gives the spider somewhere to hide if it likes. Plant a few small plants or position a few small, dead branches. Finally put a small water dish on the compost. Now you are ready to buy your tarantula, but remember to ask for a female (males will probably try and bite). When it arrives put your spider in the tank and add some wet cotton wool to the water dish. Always make sure the cotton wool is wet. Keep the tank somewhere warm and light but not in direct sunlight. Finally, feed your spider about once every week, twice a week if it eats the food quickly. You can provide most types of insects as food but beetles, grasshoppers and locusts are a suitable size. Just one a week should be enough, and if you go on holiday the tarantula will be all right, because it can do without food for over a year (but don't try making it do this, as it's cruel).

The compost and bark can be bought from most garden centres. Tarantulas, suitable tanks and their food can be bought from specialist shops which are listed at the back of the book. Surprisingly, tarantulas are very popular as pets, even if most parents aren't very fond of them. The best tarantulas for keeping as pets are those with the best tempers! These include the Mexican Blonde and Mexican Red-Leg tarantulas.

Did You Know

- Tarantulas are very good mothers. They carry their babies (called spiderlings), up to forty of them, on their backs until they are big enough to look after themselves.

- There are many different types of tarantulas including the following: Zebra tarantulas, Blonde tarantulas, Blue Front tarantulas, Black Velvet tarantulas and, would you believe it, Red Rump and Red Knee tarantulas!

- Tarantulas can live for as long as twenty-eight
  years.

17 Axolotls

In 1864 the people of Paris were the first people in Europe to see what is still one of the strangest creepy-crawlies of all. A relative of frogs and toads, this creature was found in Mexico where it was given an Aztec name meaning 'water beast'. If you're after an animal that is really weird, this could be your choice. In fact it is so weird that in a way it really doesn't exist!

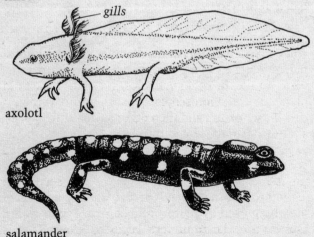

gills

axolotl

salamander

The animal is an axolotl (*axe-oh-lottle*) which is really a Mexican salamander. The only difference between an axolotl and a Mexican salamander is that for some reason the axolotl forgets to grow up. Yes, axolotls are baby Mexican salamanders and have been given their name to describe the fact that they are always going to look like the young salamander. So, axolotls aren't really a separate type of animal at all, just specially named babies.

The axolotl is related to frogs so it is an amphibian. Amphibians are important to people who study animals because they were the first animals with bones that could live on the land. Before them all the animals with bones always lived underwater, either in rivers, lakes or the sea. If the water dried up the water animals would die, so being able to live on land enabled the amphibians to walk from a place where the water had dried up to another area that was still wet. Although they were able to live on land they still had to return to water to breed, so they were half-way between land animals and water animals.

So, knowing that an axolotl is a baby amphibian you will immediately know that it is, in fact, a kind of tadpole, and in many ways you can expect it to be very similar to other tadpoles. Its diet consists of plants, at first microscopic, but as the animal grows it eats bigger plants and then other animals. In appearance it has very few surprises. It is born with the expected head, body and tail. Relatively large gills stick out on either side of the neck, looking very much like soft, pink feathers. These are used by the axolotl to obtain oxygen from the water, a method of breathing used by many animals that live in water. Quite soon the front legs begin to grow. This is probably the only surprise the young axolotl can give. Frogs, their close relatives, have tadpoles which grow their back legs first, but all newts and salamanders (don't forget we are really looking at a salamander) grow their front legs first. The other legs soon follow through and complete the changes caused by age. Certainly the axolotl gets bigger with age but it never changes shape, even though it could. In fact, if you know a friendly butcher you can try an experiment, but first you must learn how to look after the axolotl.

How To Keep Axolotls

You will need

a square fish tank or aquarium
water
axolotls (2 or 3 is best)
some fine gravel
some pond weed (*Elodea*)

What to do

Begin with a good aquarium (**but not a round one as all small, round fish tanks are very cruel because they force animals to swim in circles and this makes their backs grow crooked**). Fill this with a layer of gravel about 3cm(1–2") deep. Wash the gravel well by running water through it before you use it. Now fill the aquarium with water until it is about 3cm below the top. You can use tap water but rain, pond or river water is better. Whatever you use you must now put some plants in the aquarium. Plants are very important because they keep the water clean and full of oxygen which animals need to breathe. Most underwater plants are suitable so you can choose to buy whatever plants you find most attractive. Canadian pond weed (*Elodea*) is cheap but others will add more interest. Plant their roots in the gravel. If the aquarium is large it will be possible to include a few floating plants as well. Duckweed is easy to get and grow but fairly ordinary to look at. Frogbit (*Hydrocharis*) is a beautiful plant that looks like a tiny water-lily and is well worth having. Water ferns (*Azolla*) are equally attractive and very different. All these items can be bought from most good pet or aquarium shops.

When the plants have been put in the aquarium leave it for three weeks. If the plants die the water is poisonous and you must find water from another source. If the plants live they will add oxygen to the water and take out small amounts of poison so that it is ready for your axolotls. As with all the equipment, a good pet or aquarium shop will be able to supply your axolotls, though they may be hard to get. They will be sold to you in a plastic bag of water. Take them home and float the plastic bag in your aquarium for thirty minutes. Then open the bag and very gently tip it up so the axolotl goes into the aquarium. If your aquarium has a light, do this with the light off so the axolotl is not frightened.

Obviously you must feed the axolotl. Normally you can use fish flakes, small pieces of shrimp (soaked in water for thirty minutes and with scales removed) or live food like water fleas (*Daphnia*) or small worms (earthworms or tubifex). Of course, you'll need several axolotls if you want to breed them. If they do lay eggs you must put the eggs (there should be about 1000) in another aquarium. They will hatch after about two weeks. Axolotls can live in an unheated aquarium but will do best if kept at 60°F(17°C).

Axolotls come in two colours. The original is a dark, purple-brown which can have some darker spots. However, there is a much prettier albino form. Albino animals have no (or very little) colour. This one is pink with lovely red gills. If you prefer this type do make sure you tell the shop that you want the albino form.

Can An Axolotl Ever Grow Up?

You will need

some pig or cow thyroid	an aquarium
	one or more axolotls

What to do
As this experiment is a little more difficult, it would be a good idea to carry it out in your biology class. Set up the aquarium as just described and obtain the axolotls. What you are going to attempt to do is change the axolotl from a tadpole (salamanderpole is the proper name but it is so ugly I prefer tadpole) into an adult salamander.

Ask a friendly butcher to give you some thyroid. This is a gland that many animals have and is found in the neck. If you look in a mirror your thyroid would be under your skin at the front of your neck and it is shaped like a bow-tie. Feed small pieces of thyroid to the axolotls and remove any uneaten food after sixty minutes. Carefully look at the axolotls each day to see what they look like. It would be a good idea to record anything that happens in a notebook. The example below shows a good way of keeping your records. If you can tell the difference between your axolotls, give them names so you can describe the changes to each axolotl.

DATE	WHICH AXOLOTL	CHANGES SEEN
3 Sept. 1985	Josephine and Pinky	Fed first meal of thyroid today. They looked as if they liked it.
6 Oct. 1985	Pinky	Pinky is beginning to lose the nice pink colour.

If you keep feeding the axolotl with thyroid, it will amazingly enough suddenly remember to grow up and turn into an adult salamander. The colour will change to a rather boring brownish-green and the gills will disappear. To be honest, it's a lovely experiment but I prefer the pink, frilly axolotl to stay 'young'.

Why does thyroid make an axolotl grow up? Well, in Mexico axolotls grow in ponds and small lakes where certain chemicals are missing. The main missing chemical is iodine. When iodine is present in the water, it is absorbed by the axolotl and used by the thyroid gland to make another chemical called thyroxin (*thigh-rocks-in*). Thyroxin makes axolotls or tadpoles (and newtpoles) turn into adults. It also makes other animals like us grow up. So, instead of giving your pet axolotl iodine, you are really giving it another animal's thyroxin. The axolotl does not care whether it makes its own thyroxin or eats somebody else's.

Did You Know

- Although axolotls do not normally grow up they can still lay eggs that hatch.

- Axolotls eat their own young (in fact they eat almost anything that will fit into their mouths).

- Although an axolotl would be expected to live for ten years, they can live for as long as twenty-five years.

- Axolotls hunt by sight but they are almost blind!

Centipedes and Millipedes

Once again we can look to our friends, the arthropods (animals with a hard outer body and joints, like spiders and insects), to provide yet another group of strangely interesting creatures. These truly creepy-crawly creatures can be found almost anywhere there are dark, damp cracks, lots of nice, damp, dead leaves or plenty of rotting wood – in fact, all the perfect creepy-crawly places. Once again, though, ask anyone about them and probably the only things they will be able to tell you will be wrong.

Yes, surely everyone has heard of centipedes and millipedes, haven't they? Have you? If you have, try and answer the following questions:

1. How many legs has a centipede got?
2. How many legs has a millipede got?

Easy, wasn't it? If you ask people the same questions you usually find everyone thinks that they know the answers. What they usually tell you is that centipedes have 100 legs and millipedes have 1000 legs, but they would be wrong!

The trouble is that these animals have misleading

names. 'Cent' is a word that originally meant one hundred in Latin, so a word starting with 'cent' will probably have something to do with a hundred. For instance, CENTury means one hundred years and CENTenarian is anyone who is one hundred years or older. So, because it obviously has a lot of legs people naturally assume a CENTipede has one hundred legs. The same thing is true for millipedes because 'milli' comes from the Latin for 1000 and they look as if they have even more legs than a centipede, so people assume MILLIpedes have 1000 legs.

To find out how many legs they really do have you need to find a centipede and a millipede and count them. Try hunting in piles of dead leaves, under stones or under rotting wood. Catch them in a glass or plastic container and put a lid on it. Be careful. Centipedes can bite. You will recall that the bodies of other arthropods (relatives of centipedes and millipedes) are divided into three quite different segments – the head, thorax and abdomen. This is really obvious if you look at the shape of a wasp or bee. Now you will notice that in centipedes and millipedes the body isn't as obviously divided. They still have a head, but the rest of the body consists of a lot of segments which look almost exactly the same. If you look more closely you will find the difference between these two animals. Centipedes have *one pair* of legs on each segment. Millipedes have *two pairs* of legs on each segment. Now that might make you think that millipedes have more legs than centipedes, but that isn't necessarily true. Large centipedes with lots of segments will have more legs than small millipedes with very few segments. So the next time you are asked how many legs these animals have, remember that the only answer you can give is either one or two pairs on each segment.

Millipedes vary from being a little less than 3mm(⅛") up to 20cm(8") long, while centipedes are often slightly bigger. Despite this, many of them are avoided by other animals, including humans, because they are poisonous. Centipedes usually use their poison by injecting it into their victim with strong, sharp fangs on either side of their mouth. Giant centipede bites hurt! Although the bite is used to defend itself against large animals, it is usually used to catch and kill small animals like insects and worms which the centipede eats.

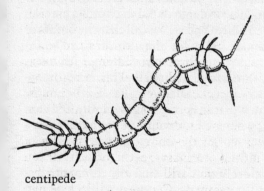

centipede

millipede

Millipedes don't bite, but don't be fooled because they are far worse. They use their poison only to protect themselves. If surprised or attacked the poison is released from tiny holes all down both sides of the body. The poison is coloured, usually brown or yellow, to put an attacker off. In case that doesn't work it is very, very smelly. The smell is a revolting mixture of bleach, cyanide and foul matter (or excrement). Can you imagine the smell of an animal that smells of two deadly poisons and also as if it has just fallen into a dirty sewer? Ugh! Wait, though, because the millipede hasn't finished. Just suppose some animal is silly enough to ignore the nasty colour and revolting smell, worse is yet to come. The bleach smell is caused by chlorine which in this mixture forms an acid. The cyanide in the mixture is prussic acid. Between them, these two deadly poisonous acids can cause any skin they contact to burn, blacken and then peel. By now you, along with most other animals, will have realized that it is best to stay away from millipedes. But even that isn't enough because some millipedes still don't feel safe and can squirt their poisons at you from up to 1m(3') away. However, they do give warning of their presence. Many of the most poisonous types can actually make their bodies glow in the dark, while others are brightly coloured, often with reds, yellows and black. Some centipedes can also give warning, either with lights or colours.

Having discovered how dangerous these creatures, especially millipedes, are, it may surprise you to learn that frogs, birds and spiders find them very tasty. The poison has no effect on them at all. For this reason there is another defence. If attacked, centipedes and millipedes will writhe and wriggle, making it very difficult to get hold of them, and sometimes also surprising the attacker enough to make it give up. If that doesn't work they can roll up into a tight ball, the hard, protective plates that cover each segment surrounding them completely. This makes them difficult to crunch, but as far as frogs are concerned it doesn't prevent them from being swallowed whole.

Centipedes and millipedes lay between 10 and 300 eggs which hatch out as tiny animals looking very similar to the adults. This is another example of incomplete metamorphosis described in the ladybird chapter. Only small changes occur as they grow from a baby into an adult. The eggs can be nearly as well protected as the adults. Some centipedes and millipedes bury the eggs or cover them with their own waste. Others will use silk, like a caterpillar or spider, to build a protective egg case or cocoon. Some even lay eggs in a nest and guard them.

How To Keep Centipedes Or Millipedes

You will need

a plastic or glass tank with lid	rotting wood and/or bark
dead leaves	potting compost
twigs	small house plants
moss	a small water bowl
cotton wool	water

with

a centipede	insects (as food)

or

millipedes	fruit and vegetable scraps

What to do

Set up the tank as described for tarantulas. Put the compost into the tank first, followed by the moss and small house plants. Then add the leaves, rotting wood, a little rotting bark and twigs. Finally position the water bowl. You are now ready to obtain the millipedes or centipedes. Don't get both unless you plan to keep them separately. Put them in the tank and fit the lid. Feed the millipedes bits of leftover raw vegetable or fruit. Centipedes need small animals like insects that you should be able to find outside. These can include worms, beetles, caterpillars, maggots and most other small creepy-crawlies. Use wet cotton wool as a water supply for both types of animal. By putting it in a water bowl it will stay wet longer. You can buy potting compost and plants from garden centres. Most of the other things can be found in gardens or the countryside.

Start your collection with small millipedes and centipedes that you can catch for yourself (with a jam jar). If you find the animals interesting, try obtaining and keeping giant tropical species. Suppliers of these and the tanks they need are listed at the back of the book. It may surprise you to learn that giant centipedes and millipedes are very popular in creepy-crawly collections.

Did You Know

- Most centipedes and millipedes grow more legs as they get older.

- 65,000,000 (sixty-five million) millipedes were seen in one migrating group in 1918 in the state of West Virginia in America. To give you some idea how many that is there are about 55,000,000 (fifty-five million) people living in the British Isles. They were probably moving to a new area to find food but nobody knows exactly why they migrate.

- Millipedes (remember that the biggest are about 20cm or 8″ long) have stopped trains. A migrating group can swarm over railway lines and when a train runs over them the millions of crushed bodies cause the wheels to slip. Since the wheels can't grip the track, the train just stops.

- When millipedes migrate they are often accompanied by centipedes and woodlice. Nobody knows why.

- Crushed millipedes have been used by Mexican Indians as poison for arrow tips.

- The greatest number of legs recorded on a millipede is 355 pairs, or a total of 710 legs.

- There is no known antidote for a centipede bite. The pain can last for three weeks. Luckily, most centipedes aren't poisonous to humans.

- Male and female millipedes attract each other by banging their heads together.

Cockroaches, other Beetles and Termites

Beetles have been mentioned several times in this book, including some that live in water, and perhaps the prettiest and most beloved of all, the ladybird. There are, of course, many other beautiful, attractive and beloved beetles, but there are also some we do not appreciate. The cockroach is one of them.

Cockroaches are pests. In Europe they are almost always found near people, either living in and near our homes or in other places we use. In tropical countries some types live near people, but others are shy and live in forests. They are pests because they are considered to be dirty, and as they live near us they can easily spoil our food, causing us to become ill. Worse still, they are very fast, there are lots of them and they are very flat. This means it is almost impossible to keep them out of the house. Attempts have been made to poison them but cockroaches quickly become resistant to poison and so it becomes useless. In fact, poisoning cockroaches has probably caused more damage to people – in the past it has definitely made large numbers of people ill.

In appearance they look like any other ordinary beetle and are often a plain brown. The babies are born looking very similar to the adults, just smaller. Although they can run very quickly (it's rare for insects to run but some beetles, termites and ants are very good at it), they can put off an attacker by emitting an awful smell. They usually have wings but are never good at flying. If they do fly, they appear to be almost out of control, and in the tropics it isn't unusual for cockroaches to fly straight into you at night with a loud bump! However, cockroaches were possibly the first animals to learn to fly. Their wings may have developed initially as protection. However they developed, it is believed they may have then been used just to glide. Eventually, the wings developed in such a way that they could move, helping cockroaches to escape their enemies. Now, many cockroaches no longer have wings. They don't need them as they are so good at running away.

In Europe they are usually found near food, so restaurants are common homes. They can also turn up in bathrooms (the German cockroach, the most common type, actually likes to eat soap) and zoos are also popular. The Oriental cockroach is unusual. It prefers an outdoor life on rubbish dumps. The East African Brown-Banded cockroach prefers to live inside televisions. Luckily, most large types live in tropical jungle, rarely being seen.

As nobody likes cockroaches, nobody wants to believe they came from their own country. For this reason the German cockroach, which is found all over Europe, is called by different names in different parts of Europe. The English call it the German cockroach. North Germans call it the Swabian cockroach (Swabian suggests Eastern Germany). East Germans call it the Russian cockroach. West Germans call it the Frenchman! Cockroaches eat just about anything, including fruit, vegetables, rotting food, wood, soap and wax.

Some other beetles are worth mentioning. Pests usually cause diseases, sting or damage our food. Beetles are very well known for destroying or damaging food. Weevils (mentioned in this book as soil animals, as many types are found in the soil) are tiny beetles, but only one needs to get into a flour store to destroy the entire contents. They breed very quickly when food is plentiful and are too small to notice until too late. Woodworms are able to damage books and furniture. This beetle lays its eggs in or on wood and paper. The little maggot that later hatches out does all the damage by boring holes in the wood and paper as it eats. Often there is no evidence of the maggot until it eats its way out and hatches into a beetle. Then, when you see the hole, it is too late because it has left behind a mass of holes inside the wood or book. The Colorado beetle is different yet again in that it eats living plants. It causes so much damage to plants that it appears on 'Wanted' posters in British airports and police stations, as if it were a deadly criminal, and much effort is concentrated on destroying it.

Perhaps the only beetle that can challenge the ladybird for the title of Queen of the beetles is the firefly. This beetle uses lights to attract males for mating. In tropical countries and warmer parts of Europe whole trees can be lit up by thousands of the little lights as the night-time mating takes place. Each type of firefly flashes its lights in a special way as a code. This makes sure only other similar fireflies come to mate with it.

Termites are not beetles so you might wonder why they are in this part of the book. The answer is that they are very close relatives of cockroaches. Although they look similar to ants, are sometimes called white ants and live in ant-like colonies, they are definitely not ants. Unlike ants the queen lives with her king all the time. They live in the dark which is why they are white; colour isn't visible in the dark. Workers do all the work, but large soldiers protect the nest which can be 6 metres (20') tall and contain millions of animals. 10,000 eggs are laid by the queen each day.

How To Build A Beetle Trap

You will need
- a jam jar
- a trowel
- 4 small stones
- a piece of slate or wood big enough to cover the top of the jar
- a garden or field

What to do

Take all your equipment out into a garden or field. Use the trowel (a small hand-held spade) to dig a hole just deep enough to hold the jam jar. Put the jar in it and fill in the gaps around the side with the loose soil. Spread out any extra soil so that it is not left in a pile. The top of the jar should now be level with the surface of the soil.

Now put the four stones on the ground around the top of the jar. Put the slate or wood on top of the stones so that it covers the jar. Make sure the slate or wood does not touch the jar or the ground. The gap will allow beetles to walk under the cover and fall into the jar.

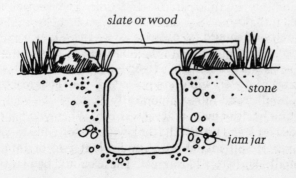

slate or wood

stone

jam jar

This sort of trap is called a pitfall trap. It will trap anything that wriggles or crawls along the ground, as well as beetles. Leave it for one night and then see what you have caught. By putting traps in different places you can find out if different beetles prefer different conditions. For instance, try putting one in an open field (or in grass) and one in a wood (or under trees).

When you have finished all your experiments, dig up the trap, fill in the hole and let any beetles you still have go back into the wild.

How To Keep A Giant Cockroach

You will need

a glass or plastic fish tank	a tank top and light
	cotton wool
water	a Giant Hissing
food	cockroach
soil	sand
small terrarium plants	a piece of bark
half a clay flower-pot	

What to do

The tank should be quite large so the Giant cockroach can move about. Fit a lid to stop it escaping. The lid should include a light. This does two things. Firstly, it lets you enjoy seeing the cockroach. Secondly, and more importantly, it keeps the cockroach healthy by providing warmth. When you have your tank and lid, fill the tank with a 6 to 8cm(2 to 3″) layer of soil mixed with sand. Plant two or three small plants to add interest. These should be plants that stay small. Any garden centre will be able to help you choose these if you ask for terrarium (or bottle garden) plants (a terrarium is a glass case for growing plants in). Also add a piece of curved bark and half a flower-pot to provide places to hide. You can now buy your Giant Hissing cockroach (suppliers are listed at the back of the book). Put it in the tank and keep it supplied with wet cotton wool and raw food. It will eat fruit or vegetables.

This cockroach is perfectly clean to keep as a pet but you should always wash your hands after handling it, just as you should with all other animals, even cats and dogs. If you intend to handle it often it is probably best if you wear gloves. This will stop you becoming sensitive to some of the chemicals in the cockroach shell.

As its name implies, this cockroach is great fun because it can make a loud hissing noise. It is also safe as it doesn't sting or bite. As long as the food you feed it is clean, the cockroach will also be as clean as many other pets.

Did You Know

- Cockroach was originally a Spanish word, *cucaracha* (*cook-uh-rah-char*).

- Cockroaches always have three of their six legs on the ground, forming a tripod so they don't fall over.

- Cockroaches were sometimes sold to tourists in the West Indies. To make this ugly creature more attractive, the tourists were told it was a 'mahogany bird'.

- Some fireflies eat other fireflies. They pretend to be interested in mating by using their lights to copy the victim's light-flash code. As soon as a firefly comes near, hoping to mate, it is pounced on and eaten.

- Over 250,000 (two hunded and fifty thousand *or* a quarter of a million) different types of beetle have been discovered.

- One of the most expensive chemicals used to make a very expensive perfume for ladies comes from squashing a beetle that lives in Vietnam. Would you try to smell nice by wearing squashed beetle?

20 Locusts, Crickets and Grasshoppers

Almost everyone likes to watch a good cartoon and Walt Disney cartoons are some of the best and most famous. Probably his most famous cartoon characters are Mickey Mouse and Donald Duck but he was responsible for many more. Just one of them was a tiny little creature known by the name of Jiminy Cricket, who was always intelligent and helpful and appeared in many cartoons to teach young people history or science. Jiminy was, as his name tells you, a cricket; one of three types of very similar creatures that are well known for their ability to jump. Very few people watch little Jiminy and realize that in real life, far from being a friend, the cricket is a pest and its relative, the locust, is one of the worst pests known to humankind.

Crickets are close relatives of grasshoppers and locusts, and all three are obviously designed to be able to jump. Their legs work in a fairly simple way. The outside of the body is hard and acts like a skeleton. This skeleton is made of a very hard substance called chitin. The insect leg bends, just as ours does, at the knee. At the back of the knee, crickets have a special kind of chitin that is slightly softer than normal. It acts just like a spring. When the insect crouches down it bends its legs and bends the spring. Now everybody knows that a bent spring just wants to become straight again, so as soon as the insect stops trying to crouch the chitin spring pushes itself straight. In doing so it straightens the leg and forces the cricket to take an enormous jump. Clever, isn't it? If you'd like to see this you can try it on yourself in the first experiment which follows.

Crickets and grasshoppers are found all over the world. They are very easy to keep as they eat any green leaves. By rubbing their legs together, they make a noise that some people like and so call it 'singing'. As they were easy to keep and also sang, the Chinese used to build little cages for them and keep them as pets. Crickets and grasshoppers were therefore popular even though they could damage crops. It is rare for too many of them to swarm together, but the same is not true of the locust.

Locusts are normally about as harmless as most other insects. They usually live alone and although they do eat green leaves, one single locust could never eat enough to cause anyone a problem. Sometimes locusts group together in millions to move to a new area. This happens about once every ten years. Imagine what millions of locusts could do, though. Think of the biggest school playing field or playground you have ever seen. Now imagine that is a field full of plants. One swarm of locusts could eat all the plants in that field in ten minutes. In tropical countries where locusts live there are usually about thirteen hours of sunlight. Can you calculate how many fields of plants a locust swarm could eat while there is some light?

The number of daylight hours = 13

One field of plants is eaten each 10 minutes.
The number of 10 minute periods in 1 hour = 6
So the number of 10 minute periods in 13 hours
= 6 × 13 = 78

So, in the daytime, one locust swarm could eat seventy-eight fields of plants!

Now can you see why a locust swarm is such a terrible pest? In Africa it has often caused famine by eating almost all of the food farmers have grown. They can even accidentally kill people. If a plane flies into a swarm of locusts, the engines can be choked by dead locusts and stop, causing the plane to crash. Luckily this is no longer a problem because the

locust

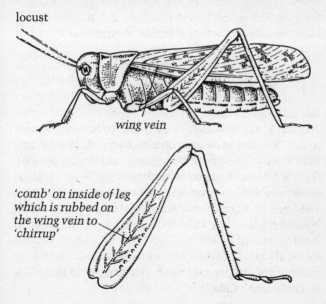

wing vein

*'comb' on inside of leg
which is rubbed on
the wing vein to
'chirrup'*

swarms can be seen on radar and planes can be kept away.

Most locusts are a dull brown or fawn in colour. A few are very brightly coloured, usually on the wings, and it is thought that this is a method of defence. The normal brown colour helps camouflage locusts when they live in the desert. If an animal attacks a group of them, the sudden jumping and flying as well as all the fluttering of the coloured wings probably baffles the attacker, giving the locust more time to get away.

Locusts attract a mate by making a 'chirping' noise. The legs have a 'comb' or a set of stiff hooks on them, and the wings have a raised line or vein running along them. The noise is made by rubbing the comb along the vein, something you can try later.

How A Cricket's Knee Helps It Jump

You will need
  a tennis ball   a chair
  your leg

What to do
Sit down in the chair. Bend your knee and put the tennis ball in the hollow behind the knee joint. Bend your knee a little more and you should be able to hold the ball without using your hands. Now, grab your ankle and pull it towards your bottom as far as you can. STOP PULLING AS SOON AS THE TEN-NIS BALL BEGINS TO HURT YOU, BUT STILL HOLD ON TO YOUR ANKLE. Let go suddenly and see what happens.

Your leg will spring back straight. This is how a cricket's leg works. Simple, isn't it?

How To Sing Like A Locust

You will need
   a piece of thick card   a comb

What to do
Rub the teeth of the comb along the edge of the card. The result should be a 'chirruping' noise similar to that which a locust makes. The comb you used is similar to that on a locust's leg. The edge of the card is like the raised vein on its wing. Making sound by rubbing two surfaces together in this way (a comb on an edge) is called stridulation (*strid-you-lay-shun*).

How To Keep Locusts

You will need

a wooden box	a thermometer
clear perspex	2 60W light bulbs
2 bulb holders	insulated electric wire
2 electric plugs	a thermostat
a metal (or plastic) tube	sand
at least 5cm(2") wide	cotton wool
and 12cm(5") long	grass and green leaves
with one end sealed	2 small clasps to hold
wire mesh	lids closed
water	saw
4 small hinges	screwdriver
screws for hinges, etc.	drill and bits
electric drill	some strong twigs

Keeping locusts is quite easy but this is the most difficult cage to build of all those described in the book. You will need help and should ask an adult who is good at building things. You might be able to persuade one of your teachers to build this for the school.

Make a wooden box that resembles the one shown in the diagram. It should be approximately 30cm × 30cm × 50cm(12″ × 12″ × 20″) tall. Looking from the front there should be a shelf approximately 15–20cm (6–8″) up from the base and made of wood. The shelf must have a hole cut in it to hold the metal tube. The tube needs to be at least 5cm(2″) wide, 12cm(5″) long and sealed at one end. It should be positioned in either of the two front corners of the shelf so the rim is level with the shelf top. The open end of the tube should be at the top. The bulk of the tube will extend into the lower compartment where a bulb will be fitted to heat it. The top of the box should be hinged to make a lid. The front of the box should be made in two parts. The area below the shelf should be made of wood and fitted as a hinged door. Above the shelf the front should be made of clear perspex so that you can see inside. Cut a hole in the lid and cover this with the wire mesh so that air can move freely in and out of the cage.

The two bulb holders with their bulbs must now be fitted. One should be positioned on the inside, at the very top of the back of the box so that it heats up and lights the locusts. The wiring goes directly to a plug which will later be inserted into a power socket. Make sure the bulb will not be closer to the lid than about 3cm(1″). The second bulb unit is fitted in the lower section (below the shelf) in the centre of the back. The wiring for this unit must go through the thermostat before being attached to a plug.

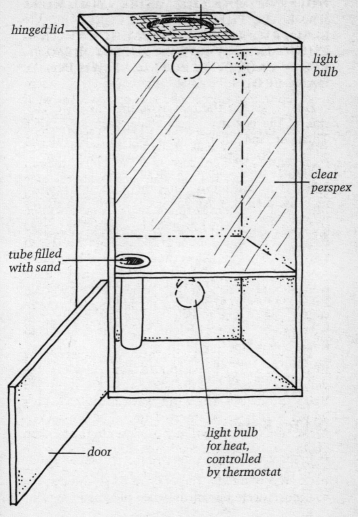

wire mesh covering air hole

hinged lid

light bulb

clear perspex

tube filled with sand

door

light bulb for heat, controlled by thermostat

IF AN EXPERT IN ELECTRICAL WORK
DOES NOT DO THIS WORK, YOU MUST
HAVE ALL THE WIRING CHECKED BY AN
ELECTRICIAN BEFORE PLUGGING ANY-
THING INTO A POWER SUPPLY. REMEM-
BER – FAULTY ELECTRICAL WIRING IS
DANGEROUS.

Finally, set the thermostat so that the lower section of the box never gets colder than 80°F(28°C).
Then put sand into the metal tube until it is full and
add a few strong twigs for the locusts to climb on.

You are now ready to keep the locusts. If you are
lucky they will breed using the deep, hot sand to
incubate their eggs. All you need do now is to always
provide wet cotton wool and food. Grass or other
green leaves will be ideal. Try to add different types of
leaf from time to time.

Locusts can be bought from some pet shops,
especially those that sell lizards and snakes. Some
suppliers are also listed at the back of the book. If you
cannot get anyone to help you build the cage, you
have two other ways of doing this. The easiest is to
forget about breeding them and just use a large fish
tank. Leave out the sand. Alternatively, a school
teacher should be able to buy a locust breeding cage
from a school biological supplier.

Did You Know

- In the days when China was ruled by an Emperor,
  all the ruling families had pet crickets.

- Locusts were one of the great plagues of ancient
  Egypt.

- The mole-cricket is specially adapted for digging with its front legs, which are larger than those of other crickets and are flattened to help scoop out soil.

- Bush crickets crawl rather than jump or fly. Branches would get in their way if they tried to jump or flutter.

- Jiminy Cricket first appeared in the Walt Disney cartoon *Pinocchio*.

21 Stick Insects, Leaf Insects and Praying Mantis

Finally, although there are thousands of other creepy-crawlies left to describe, here are three that are so incredible it would be a shame not to mention them. They are masters of disguise and, unlike all the other animals we looked at, are designed to remain still. Well, not quite still.

Stick insects are exactly what they sound like – insects that look like sticks. They are generally long thin animals on six legs. They are brilliantly designed to avoid being eaten. They are shaped like sticks and are usually the colour of the stick they most like to live on. They also pose so as to confuse an enemy. The body is held so one end touches the branch it is standing on and the other end points outward like a real twig. Then some of the legs (all of which look like tiny twigs) are held out to look more like twigs. Finally, the insect stays absolutely motionless or sways slightly as if it were a twig in a breeze. All in all, it can really confuse almost any enemy.

Leaf insects are even more incredible. Instead of looking like a stick they are designed to look like a leaf. Their wide, very flat bodies even have the markings of a leaf, including the centre rib and side veins.

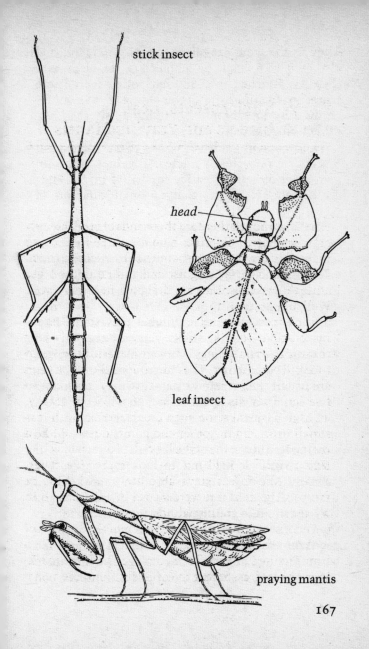

stick insect

head

leaf insect

praying mantis

They are the same size, shape and colour as a leaf, and also manage to stand on a branch so they look as if they are attached to it like any other leaf. These fantastic creatures are better designed to confuse animals by looking like something else, than any other living animal.

By now you might have guessed that stick and leaf insects are very closely related. Together they form a group of insects called Phasmids (*fas-mids*). They are harmless creatures that eat small amounts of plants.

The Praying Mantis is not quite as harmless. In fact, a mantis would quite happily eat any stick or leaf insect it could find. Yes, they are carnivorous and so eat animals. They are also brilliantly disguised to look like parts of a plant, but it isn't to help them get away from hungry animals. Imagine you went for a walk and saw a shop full of things you wanted to buy. In you walked and suddenly you realized you had walked into a large, hungry mouth, cleverly disguised to look like a shop! Well, luckily shops don't get hungry, but the mantis does and it waits, pretending to be something else, for supper to walk by. Then, zap! Out flash the long arms to catch the unlucky animal, quickly dragging it back to its jaws to be slowly eaten alive.

The mantis looks very like a grasshopper. The main difference is that its head is shaped like a triangle. The mouthparts are also different, being very agile to bite and chew their prey. The mantis is from an insect group called Mantids (*man-tids*). European mantids are long and thin. Tropical mantids can be quite short and fat. They come in many more colours than grasshoppers, leaf or stick insects, and have well-developed wings to fly to new hunting areas.

How To Keep Phasmids Or Mantids

You will need

a glass or plastic aquarium	phasmids *or* mantids
soil	an aquarium lid with a fitted light
small (terrarium) plants	sand
food	cotton wool
	strong twigs

What to do

Begin by filling the aquarium with a 5–6cm(2″) layer of soil and sand. Add some small plants for interest and a few strong twigs on which the animals can live. If you buy a praying mantis, buy just one. If you want more, tell the supplier why and you will be advised if it is sensible to put more than one in a cage. Two together might try to eat each other! If you want phasmids, you can buy several stick insects, leaf insects or some of both to keep together. DO NOT PUT PHASMIDS AND MANTIDS TOGETHER. The mantids will eat almost any other insect.

Put the insects in the aquarium and put a good lid on it. Feed phasmids with fresh leaves and perhaps try a little fruit. Feed mantids with live insects such as beetles, moths and flies. Keep tropical insects warm all year. If they are kept indoors in a centrally heated house, they will be all right if the temperature is always above 60°F. Otherwise, when you buy the aquarium, also ask for a thermostat and heater suitable for a vivarium (a dry tank).

All these animals are safe to handle but wash your hands afterwards. If you handle them often it is best to wear gloves so their skin doesn't irritate your hands. Suppliers of these insects are listed at the back of the book.

Did You Know

- Some stick insects and leaf insects can change colour to match their surroundings. This is a very rare ability among animals. The two other animals famous for being able to do this really well are chameleons, a type of lizard, and cuttlefish, which are similar to octopus and squid and are related to snails.

- Leaf and stick insects can grow a new leg if one is broken off. This is also a very rare ability among animals.

- The Maltese mantis is pink. It hides in pink orchid flowers waiting for flies and butterflies to come by.

- Stick insects can be found wild in England. Their location is kept secret to protect them, as they are now very rare.

Suppliers

Shops In Britain That Sell Creepy-Crawlies Directly Or By Post

Shops that sell live animals are different from most other shops. After all, you can't store live animals in cans on a shelf as in a supermarket. So no good pet shop can always promise to have the animals you want. The shops listed below all specialize in creepy-crawlies, but you should always write or phone before visiting them or sending any money for the animals you want.

In some places you may need special permission to keep animals. Do ask the shop if you need a licence *before* you buy. The local police or zoos should also be able to tell you about licences.

Finally, think very carefully before you buy animals that can hurt. For example, tarantulas can give a painful bite if handled badly. If you buy one you may have to put up with occasional bad temper. Worse still are dangerous animals. None is listed in this book but shops do sell them. DO NOT BUY OR KEEP DANGEROUS ANIMALS. They are best left to experts and zoos. Always ask the shop to advise you if your choice is dangerous. Remember, once you have bought the animal you must look after it. They are all living creatures, not toys, and they must not be neglected or mistreated.

Pet Fare	18 Hare Hill Road, Littleborough, Lancs. (0706) 78452	Frogs, toads, spiders, pet food, accessories.
Entomological Livestock Supplies	Unit 3, Beaver Park, Hayseech Road, Halesowen, West Midlands B63 3PZ (021) 550 0180	Butterflies, praying mantis, leaf insects, giant moths, stick insects, tarantulas, locusts, cages, books, accessories.
Exotic Animals	114 Broadway, Didcot, Oxon. (0235) 811306	Frogs, toads, newts, tarantulas, other spiders, centipedes, millipedes, giant snails, stick insects, praying mantis, giant hissing cockroaches, pet food, books, cages, accessories.
The Vivarium	55 Boundary Road, Walthamstow, London E17 (01) 520 2072	Frogs, toads, newts, salamanders, axolotls, cages, accessories.

Paul Sullivan	34 Willow Avenue, Torquay (0803) 312564	Frogs, tarantulas, pet food, accessories.
Geofron Breeding Centre	Llangibi, Gwynedd, Wales LL53 7UP (076688) 480	Crickets, cages.
S.W.V.L. Livefoods	7 Pounds Park, Bere Alston, Yelverton, Devon PL20 7AY (0822) 840178	Specialist amphibian food supplier.

In addition to the addresses listed above you may be able to find other suppliers from the magazines *Exchange and Mart* and *Aquarist (and pondkeeper)*, and from:

The Amateur Entomologists Society, A.E.S. Registrar, 355 Hounslow Road, Hanworth, Feltham, Middlesex

(Enclose a stamped, addressed envelope.)

There are also specialist societies for people interested in keeping frogs and toads, butterflies and moths or tarantulas. Your local library should be able to help you contact them. Always let societies know your age when writing to them.

Shops In Britain Specializing In Supplies For Ponds Directly Or By Post

Several of the creepy-crawlies described in this book can be kept in a garden pond. The following shops supply everything necessary to build a pond, plants and animals to make it interesting and plenty of good advice. Everything, including the plants and animals, can be bought by post but do make sure you read any advice the shop sends you before you order anything. For price lists and advice write, enclosing a cheque or postal order for fifty-pence.

Stapeley Water
Gardens Ltd,
92 London Road,
Stapeley,
Nantwich,
Cheshire,
CW5 7LH
0270 623868

Maydencroft
Aquatic
Nurseries,
Gosmore,
Nr. Hitchin,
Herts.
SG4 7QD
0462 56020

Matlock Garden
Waterlife
Centre Ltd,
Nottingham Road,
Tansley,
Matlock,
Derby., DE4 5FR
0629 4221

Microscope Suppliers

Very expensive microscopes are not essential for looking at creepy-crawlies. Almost any microscope will allow you to see fascinating creatures that are too small to see otherwise.

In general, two types of microscope are useful. One type can be carried in the pocket and is useful for looking at creatures without having to take them home with you. At home, a larger and more powerful microscope will let you see more detail.

Suitable microscopes can be bought from good toy or hobby shops. Listed below are the names of some microscope manufacturers. If you cannot find any of the products mentioned, write directly to the manufacturer (or distributor) asking for details of your nearest stockist. Enclose a stamped, addressed envelope (or two international reply coupons, available at post offices, if writing to or from another country).

Edu Science	distributed by Laslo Tamaron, Rochelle Park, NJ 07666 USA	Microscope sets, slide kits, prepared slides of creepy-crawlies.
Salter Science	Salter Science, Glenrothes, Fife, Scotland	Junior microscopes, microscope/ telescope (pocket).
Humbrol	Humbrol Ltd, Marfleet, Hull HU9 5NE	Pocket microscope, slide-making kit.

Places to Visit

The following list gives addresses of places in Britain that keep live creepy-crawlies for you to look at. Some, including a few of the butterfly farms, will even let you walk in the same room as the animals and it is possible to watch while a giant butterfly lands on your arm to take a rest.

Always write or phone before trying to visit any of the places listed below. Some may shut during the winter.

London Zoo, Regents Park, London NW1 4RY

Edinburgh Butterfly Farm, Dobbies Garden Centre, Lasswade, Nr. Edinburgh, Midlothian
(031) 663 4932

London Butterfly Farm, Syon Park, Brentford, Middlesex
(01) 560 7272

Stratford Butterfly Farm, Tramway Walk, Stratford-upon-Avon, Warwickshire
(0789) 292048

Weymouth Butterfly Farm, Lodmoor Country Park, Greenhill, Weymouth, Dorset
(0305) 783311

Protecting Creepy-Crawlies

If you have enjoyed reading this book, then you will want to make sure there are always plenty of creepy-crawlies left in the world. Apart from being interesting, many are beautiful, and all of them are important, including the ugly or poisonous ones. After all, just think how many flies there would be if we killed all the spiders that normally eat them.

You can help protect the animals in several ways. First, always be careful with live animals, and if you want to study them make sure you put them back where you found them as soon as possible. Second, join a conservation society in your local area. These are groups of people who care about wild animals (and plants) and who will not only tell you how you can help, but can also show you many more amazing things that live or grow near you. Ask your library how you can contact your local group. Third, if you live in Britain, you can adopt a creepy-crawly. London Zoo keeps many different animals. For a small amount of money you can make sure that some creepy-crawlies are fed and kept healthy for other people to see and enjoy. In return the zoo will let you visit your adopted creepy-crawly free of charge, and they will also put up a sign to say how you are helping them. Perhaps you might like to get a group of friends or your class at school to be adopters.

If you would like to adopt one or more creepy-crawlies, write to the London Zoo, Regents Park, London NW1 4RY and ask for an Adopt an Animal application form.

Index

183